READING GROUP CHOICES
2021

Selections for lively discussions

Reading Group Choices' goal is to join with publishers, bookstores, libraries, trade associations, and authors to develop resources to enhance the shared reading group experience. *Reading Group Choices* is distributed annually to bookstores, libraries, and directly to book groups. Titles included in the current and previous issues are posted on ReadingGroupChoices.com. Books presented here have been recommended by book group members, librarians, booksellers, literary agents, publicists, authors, and publishers. All submissions are then reviewed to ensure the discussibility of each title. Once a title is approved for inclusion, publishers are asked to underwrite production costs so that copies of *Reading Group Choices* can be distributed for a minimal charge. For additional copies, you can place an order through our online store, contact us, or contact your local library or bookstore. For more information, please visit our website at **ReadingGroupChoices.com.**

Cover art, *Marcus Books* by Jenny Kroik (2020) https://www.jennykroik.com/
Design by Sarah Jane Boecher

Copyright © 2020 Reading Group Choices LLC

All Rights Reserved.

Published in the United States by Reading Group Choices LLC

ISBN 9781733268325

For further information, contact:
Reading Group Choices
info@ReadingGroupChoices.com
ReadingGroupChoices.com

PRAISE FOR *READING GROUP CHOICES*

"We have learned over the years that displays are a great way to encourage circulation at our small, rural library. One of our best displays is based on the wonderful literary guide published by Reading Group Choices! ... Patrons cannot wait to get their copies and start reading. We sincerely LOVE your product and feel that it helps us create one of our favorite displays EVER."
—**Gail Nartker, Sandusky District Library**

"Reading Group Choices continues to be a first-rate guide for those delicious reads that book group members enjoy reading, and that prompt the most enriching discussions." —**Donna Paz Kaufman, Paz & Associates, The Bookstore Training Group**

"I recommend Reading Group Choices as the number one starting point for book clubs. The newsletter is fantastic, and I especially like the Spotlight Book Club section. It is a nice way to meet other book clubs. I am very happy with the book selections offered by Reading Group Choices. Thank you for this excellent service." —**Ana Martin, Cover to Cover Book Club, Hollywood, FL**

"Not only is Reading Group Choices a great resource for individual readers and book groups, it's also an invaluable tool for teachers looking to introduce new books into their curriculum. Reading Group Choices is a brilliant concept, well executed." —**Kathleen Rourke, Executive Director of Educational Sales and Marketing, Candlewick Press**

"I love your book, website and the newsletters! As an organizer of two book clubs, it's so great to get an early line on upcoming titles. The hardest part is waiting so long to read the book! By using recommendations from your newsletters, I can build a list of monthly book selections one whole year in advance." —**Marcia, CCSI Book Club**

"Quail Ridge Books has worked with Reading Group Choices for many years and the guide has been sought out at our twice yearly Book Club Bash. The prize bags of books have been a highlight. We are great partners in getting good books into the hands of people who love to read and discuss books."
—**René Martin, Events Coordinator, Quail Ridge Books**

Welcome to

READING GROUP
CHOICES

"Books are a form of political action. Books are knowledge. Books are reflection. Books change your mind."

"Writing is really a way of thinking – not just feeling but thinking about things that are disparate, unresolved, mysterious, problematic or just sweet."

—**Toni Morrison** (1931-2019)

Dear Readers,

Welcome to the 27th edition of Reading Group Choices! In what has been a challenging year, it is wonderful to see how creative and industrious book groups have become to meet virtually or physically distanced, and how many are reconsidering their approach to choosing books to find a new standard for equal distribution of authors across race and gender.

This time has reconfirmed our belief in the importance of discussing literature and sharing opinions. Book groups are not just about books, but about the relationships we share with our fellow readers. We are so pleased we can continue offering support and suggestions.

The 27th edition includes a variety of fiction, nonfiction, and young adult titles. From historical novels and nonfiction that give voice to unrecognized and underrepresented people, to middle-grade books that engage timely social issues, we chose titles to inspire thoughtful and important discussions across genre and subject matter. Some books are available now and some will be available in 2021 so you can plan ahead.

There are longer versions of the conversation starters in this volume available online in our searchable database, along with author interviews and excerpts. Be sure to sign up for our eNewsletter, where you can find out about new monthly recommendations and giveaways as well as other resources for your groups.

To order more copies of this edition or past editions, visit our store online at www.ReadingGroupChoices.com.

Thank you to all of our readers who inspire us to keep finding and recommending new books. We hope you enjoy another year of reading, sharing, and discovering new favorites. Here's to finding other worlds and stories to get lost in and continuing the conversation through all modes of discussion!

Mary Morgan
Reading Group Choices

Contents

FICTION

After Francesco, Brian Malloy..12

Afterlife, Julia Alvarez 14

American Gospel, Lin Enger..16

The Bear, Andrew Krivak 18

The Bitch, Pilar Quintana 20

The Book of CarolSue, Lynne Hugo 22

Churchill's Secret Messenger, Alan Hlad 24

Cilka's Journey, Heather Morris..26

Dear Miss Kopp: A Kopp Sisters Novel, Amy Stewart............28

Every Bone a Prayer, Ashley Blooms 30

A Girl Is a Body of Water, Jennifer Nansubuga Makumbi 32

Lady Clementine, Marie Benedict 34

The Last Days of Ellis Island, Gaëlle Josse.........................36

The Last Flight, Julie Clark 38

My Dark Vanessa, Kate Elizabeth Russell 40

Nothing to See Here, Kevin Wilson 42

Our Riches, Kaouther Adimi...44

The Paris Children: A Novel of WWII, Gloria Goldreich...........46

The Southern Book Club's Guide to Slaying Vampires,
Grady Hendrix 48

The Streel: A Deadwood Mystery, Mary Logue 50

Telephone, Percival Everett..52

When the Apricots Bloom, Gina Wilkinson........................54

Wild Women and the Blues, Denny S. Bryce 56

The Wondrous and Tragic Life of Ivan and Ivana, Maryse Condé ...58

NONFICTION

American Harvest: God, Country, and Farming in the Heartland, Marie Mutsuki Mockett.........62

Brave Enough, Jessie Diggins.........64

The Dragons, the Giant, the Women: A Memoir, Wayétu Moore.....66

Hudson Bay Bound: Two Women, One Dog, Two Thousand Miles to the Arctic, Natalie Warren.........68

Me and White Supremacy: Combat Racism, Change the World, and Become a Good Ancestor, Layla F. Saad.........70

No Visible Bruises: What We Don't Know About Domestic Violence Can Kill Us, Rachel Louise Snyder.........72

Overground Railroad: The Green Book and the Roots of Black Travel in America, Candacy Taylor.........74

The Witch of Eye: Essays, Kathryn Nuernberger.........76

Women Rowing North: Navigating Life's Currents and Flourishing As We Age, Mary Pipher.........78

The Yellow House: A Memoir, Sarah M. Broom.........80

YOUNG ADULT

All Thirteen: The Incredible Cave Rescue of the Thai Boys' Soccer Team, Christina Soontornvat.........84

Black Brother, Black Brother, Jewell Parker Rhodes.........86

The Burning, Laura Bates.........88

Clean Getaway, Nic Stone.........90

Firekeeper's Daughter, Angeline Boulley.........92

Mad, Bad & Dangerous to Know, Samira Ahmed.........94

On These Magic Shores, Yamile Saied Méndez.........96

One of the Good Ones, Maika Moulite and Maritza Moulite.........98

The Silver Arrow, Lev Grossman.........100

Stamped: Racism, Antiracism, and You, Jason Reynolds and Ibram X. Kendi.........102

They Went Left, Monica Hesse *104*
This Is My America, Kim Johnson *106*
Trowbridge Road, Marcella Pixley *108*
The Watsons Go to Birmingham -- 1963, Christopher Paul Curtis . . *110*
What Makes Us, Rafi Mittlefehldt. *112*

FICTION

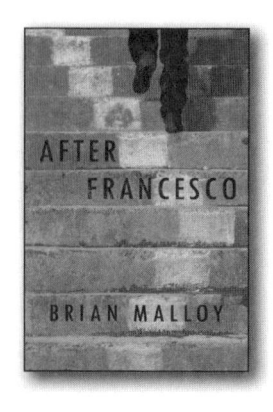

AFTER FRANCESCO
Brian Malloy

Set in New York City and Minneapolis at the peak of the AIDS crisis, *After Francesco* is both a tribute to a generation lost to the pandemic and a universally powerful exploration of heartbreak, recovery, and the ways in which love can defy grief ...

The year is 1988 and 28-year-old Kevin Doyle is bone-tired of attending funerals. It's been two years since his partner Francesco died from AIDS, an epidemic ravaging New York City and going largely ignored by a government that expects those effected to suffer in silence; to feel unjustifiable shame and guilt on top of their loss.

Some people might insist that Francesco and the other friends he's lost to the disease are in a better place, but Kevin definitely isn't. Half-alive, he spends his days at a mind-numbing job and nights with the ghost of Francesco, drunk and drowning in memories of a man who was too young to die.

When Kevin hits an all-time low, he realizes it's time to move back home to Minnesota and figure out how to start living again—without Francesco. With the help of a surviving partners support group and friends both old and new, Kevin slowly starts to do just that. But an unthinkable family betrayal, and the news that his best friend is fighting for his life in New York, will force a reckoning and a defining choice.

ABOUT THE AUTHOR: **Brian Malloy** is an award-winning author and activist. The recipient of ALA's Alex Award and the Minnesota Book Award, his novels also have been shortlisted for The Violet Quill Award and the Ferro-Grumley Award for LGBT fiction. An early employee of the Minnesota AIDS Project, Malloy helped organize the state's first AIDS Walk in 1988. He received his MFA from the University of Minnesota and currently teaches creative writing. Visit him at MalloyWriter.com.

May 2021 | Hardcover | $26.00 | 9781496733511 | Kensington Books

CONVERSATION STARTERS

1. *After Francesco* opens with a quote from Vito Russo, a gay film historian and author who died of AIDS in 1990. What meaning do you take from Russo's statement that AIDS is "like living through a war which is happening only for those people who happen to be in the trenches"?

2. Have you experienced the death of one or more people that you loved deeply? How did the immediate impact of their loss feel different from the longer-term impact?

3. Many of the events depicted in *After Francesco* are real. Were you familiar with ACT UP's actions at the F.D.A and Trump Tower, the first Minnesota AIDS Walk, or the Tompkins Square Park riot? Did you prefer ACT UP's civil disobedience or the AIDS Walk in terms of how best to address the AIDS crisis?

4. Francesco's sister-in-law defends her fabricated memoir by claiming it's doing good by raising AIDS awareness and changing hearts and minds. Do you agree? Why do you think she wrote the book?

5. What role does religion play in *After Francesco*? Do Aunt Nora, Father Michael, and Kevin share any common ground when it comes to faith?

6. In 2018, *New York Times* writer Kurt Soller addressed the newspaper's AIDS coverage: "Information about the spread of illness was often scant, judgmental or distressingly vague… often buried in the back of the newspaper, far from national news stories that were deemed important enough for the front page." Did the media's failure to cover the crisis contribute to the spread of HIV?

7. There are two depictions of assisted dying (also called assisted suicide) in *After Francesco*. Assisted dying is now legal and regulated in Oregon and Washington. Should assisted dying be expanded to the rest of the country? Why or why not?

8. Kevin comes to think of his grief as a selfish kind of grief, one that he had to stop hoarding like food during a blight. Did you find his grief selfish? Why or why not?

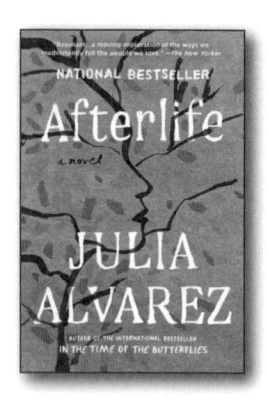

AFTERLIFE
Julia Alvarez

The first adult novel in fifteen years by the internationally bestselling author of *In the Time of the Butterflies* and *How the García Girls Lost Their Accents*

Antonia Vega, the immigrant writer at the center of *Afterlife*, has had the rug pulled out from under her. She has just retired from the college where she taught English when her beloved husband, Sam, suddenly dies. And then more jolts: her bighearted but unstable sister disappears, and Antonia returns home one evening to find a pregnant, undocumented teenager on her doorstep. Antonia has always sought direction in the literature she loves—lines from her favorite authors play in her head like a soundtrack—but now she finds that the world demands more of her than words.

Set in this political moment of tribalism and distrust, *Afterlife* asks: What do we owe those in crisis in our families, including—maybe especially—members of our human family? How do we live in a broken world without losing faith in one another or ourselves? And how do we stay true to those glorious souls we have lost?

"A gorgeously intimate portrait of an immigrant writer ... carving out hope." —*O, The Oprah Magazine*

"A beautifully written novel with a timely theme." —*People*

"Alvarez crafts a moving portrait of the lengths people will go to help one another in moments of uncertainty." —*Time*

"A stunning work of art." —**Elizabeth Acevedo**

ABOUT THE AUTHOR: **Julia Alvarez** left the Dominican Republic for the United States in 1960. She is the author of six novels, three books of nonfiction, three collections of poetry, and eleven books for children and young adults. She has taught and mentored writers in schools and communities across America and, until her retirement in 2016, was a writer-in-residence at Middlebury College. Her novel *In the Time of the Butterflies* was selected by the National Endowment for the Arts for its national Big Read program. In 2013, President Obama awarded Alvarez the National Medal of Arts in recognition of her extraordinary storytelling.

April 2020 | Hardcover | $25.95 | 9781643750255 | Algonquin Books
April 2021 | Paperback | $16.95 | 9781643751368 | Algonquin Books

CONVERSATION STARTERS

1. Antonia and her sisters are close and clearly love one another; at the same time, like many siblings, they argue, put each other in boxes, and are not always supportive. How are the sisters similar and how are they different? Which parts of their relationships felt familiar to you, if you have siblings?

2. Antonia notes that in many ways, her husband, Sam, remains alive in her head: she often wonders what he would say or do, and she lets that guide her actions. Do you think Antonia would have made different decisions about Mario, Estela, and Izzy if Sam had still been alive?

3. How do you feel about the actions Antonia ultimately takes to help Mario and Estela? Does their story change your thinking about immigration in America? If so, how?

4. Discuss the sisters' plan to get help for Izzy and the ways that it backfired. What do you think about how they handled the situation?

5. The sisters all have distinct roles in the sisterhood, and Antonia also had a defined role in her relationship with Sam (bad cop to his good cop). How did Sam's death change the way Antonia viewed herself? How do you think Izzy's death will alter the roles of the sisterhood? What is your role in your own family? Is it accurate, fair?

6. Antonia is often viewed as the selfish sister. Despite this, she struggles with recognizing and asking for what she needs. In *Afterlife*, she is frequently called on to assist others. How do you think this helps her better understand her own needs?

7. Antonia frequently recites lines from her favorite authors and poets, and their words provide comfort and wisdom. Do you have poems, songs, books, or other stories that you return to when you need comfort? How have the arts helped you in a dark time?

8. When we have identified an injustice or problem in our world or in our family, do we have a responsibility to address it? Antonia remembers a Tolstoy story with three questions: *What is the best time to do things? Who is the most important one? What is the right thing to do?* How do you decide the balance between taking care of yourself and taking care of others?

9. Who in this book has an afterlife?

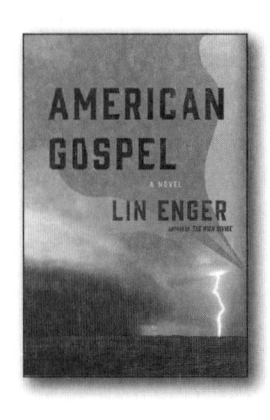

AMERICAN GOSPEL
Lin Enger

On a small farm beside a lake in Minnesota's north woods an old man is waiting for the Rapture, which God has told him will happen in two weeks, on August 19, 1974. When word gets out, Last Days Ranch becomes ground zero for The End, drawing zealots, curiosity seekers, and reporters—among them the prophet's son, a skeptical New York writer suddenly caught between his overbearing father and the news story of a lifetime, and Melanie Magnus, a glamorous actress who has old allegiances to both father and son.

Writing with clear compassion and gentle wit, Lin Enger draws us into these disparate yet inextricably linked lives. Set during a time that resonates with our own tension-filled moment, *American Gospel* cuts close to the battles occurring within ourselves and for the soul of the nation, and in doing so radiates light on a dark strain in America's psyche, when the false security of dogma competes with the risky tumult of freedom.

"No one illuminates father–son relationships better than Lin Enger. He masterfully weaves a deeply moving and unforgettable story about faith, ambition, and the tangled threads that bind family and community. Wise and lyrical, American Gospel *kept me spellbound from the first word to the last."*
—**Ann Weisgarber, author of** *The Personal History of Rachel DuPree* **and** *The Glovemaker*

"A tightly constructed novel in which unexpected second chances lead to forgiveness, lost and found families, and enlightenment. American Gospel *is tenderly written, expertly plotted, and culminates in an ending for the ages. A wonderful book."* —**Nickolas Butler, author of** *Shotgun Lovesongs* **and** *Little Faith*

*"*American Gospel *is a marvel. Long after its exciting climax, the captivating characters, vivid images, and provocative themes are sure to linger with readers."* —**Larry Watson, author of** *Montana 1948*

ABOUT THE AUTHOR: **Lin Enger** has published two previous novels, *Undiscovered Country* and *The High Divide*, a finalist for awards from the Midwest Booksellers Association, the Society of Midland Authors, and Reading the West. His stories have been published in literary journals such as *Glimmer Train*, *Ascent*, and *American Fiction*.

October 2020 | Hardcover | $24.95 | 9781517910549 | University of Minnesota Press

CONVERSATION STARTERS

1. Who is the main character in this novel? Which one has the most to gain or lose? For whom do you feel the most sympathy?

2. In what ways—culturally and politically—is 1974 a mirror of the present moment?

3. What does Enoch's prophecy mean to Melanie Magnus? What makes theirs such a complicated connection? Do you think Melanie will go back to her life in Hollywood?

4. Considering the way he was raised and his conflicts with Enoch, what are Peter's strengths and weaknesses? What factors seem to motivate the decisions he makes?

5. The killing of the lion is an important incident in both Enoch's life and Peter's. How do the two men see it differently? How does the lion's significance evolve?

6. Compare Melanie's relationships with Morris and with Peter. Compare Peter's relationships with Joanie and with Melanie. Do you think Melanie and Peter have a future together?

7. In terms of place, people, and culture, does the novel resonate with what you know about rural Minnesota, or rural mid-America?

8. Discuss the roles of Victor Stubblefield and Skinny Magnussen, both of whom are outcasts in their own ways. How are these two characters alike and different?

9. Why do Enoch and Sylvie, apparently so dissimilar in their beliefs, seem to have such a strong bond?

10. Why is fifteen-year old Willie the one who must finally take the lead in trying to save Enoch from the potentially damaging consequences of his prophecy? Why did no one else think of taking control of the situation?

11. What are your thoughts on the state of Enoch's mental health? In the final analysis, is he a character who does more harm than good, or vice versa?

12. How does *American Gospel* fit into the genre of apocalyptic/post-apocalyptic literature? Does it remind you of other novels in this genre?

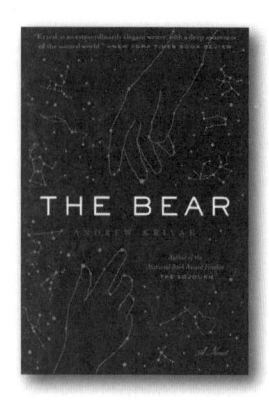

THE BEAR
Andrew Krivak

LibraryReads Pick

hoopla Book Club Spotlight Selection

From National Book Award finalist Andrew Krivak comes a fable of Earth's last two human inhabitants and a girl's journey home

In an Edenic future, a girl and her father live close to the land in the shadow of a lone mountain. They possess a few remnants of civilization: some books, a pane of glass, a set of flint and steel, a comb. The father teaches the girl how to fish and hunt, the secrets of the seasons and the stars. He is preparing her for an adulthood in harmony with nature, for they are the last of humankind. But when the girl finds herself alone in an unknown landscape, it is a bear that will lead her back home through a vast wilderness that offers the greatest lessons of all, if she can only learn to listen.

"Lyrical ... Gorgeous ... Krivak's serene and contemplative novel invites us to consider a vision of time as circular, of existence as grand and eternal beyond the grasp of individuals—and of a world able to outlive human destructiveness." —*Washington Post*

"[A] tender apocalyptic fable ... endowed with such fullness of meaning that you have to assign this short, touching book its own category: the post-apocalypse utopia." —*Wall Street Journal*

"Exquisite ... More than a parable for our times, it's a call to listen to the world around us before it's too late." —*Observer*

ABOUT THE AUTHOR: **Andrew Krivak** is the author of *The Bear*, *The Signal Flame*, and *The Sojourn*, a National Book Award finalist and winner of both the Chautauqua Prize and Dayton Literary Peace Prize. He lives with his wife and three children in Somerville, Massachusetts, and Jaffrey, New Hampshire, in the shadow of Mount Monadnock, which inspired much of the landscape in *The Bear*.

February 2020 | Paperback | $16.99 | 9781942658702 | Bellevue Literary Press

CONVERSATION STARTERS

1. From the very first sentence, we're aware that this will be a novel that grapples with human extinction. How do the father and his daughter, described as "the last two," view their place in the world? Why are they unnamed?

2. In an interview with *Library Journal*, the novel's editor observed, "While we don't ever learn what cataclysm occurred to undermine the human species, it's hard to read the book without thinking of our fears about climate change." Why do you think the author chose not to be explicit about what happened in the past?

3. Early in the novel, the girl watches a bear emerge from the woods and walk toward the lake. She asks her father, "Was my mother a bear?" Why does she pose this question? What roles do animals play in the novel?

4. Did the story change the way you experience nature or think about the creatures of the natural world?

5. The book provides a great deal of insight and authentic detail about gathering and preparing food, making clothing, and finding shelter in the wilderness. In that way, it serves as a physical survival guide. But in what ways does it also serve as a spiritual survival guide?

6. In a moving passage, the girl receives the following advice: "You need to be hungry for more than food. More than sleep. We all go to sleep and will be asleep for a long time. Be hungry for what you have yet to do while you're awake." How does the girl process this advice?

7. In what way does the novel examine feelings of loneliness and grief?

8. How would you classify *The Bear*? Is it a coming of age story? A fable? Utopian or dystopian?

9. Although *The Bear* was written for adults, does it remind you of any of your favorite childhood books?

10. How did you feel after finishing *The Bear*? Did the ending surprise you? Was there a particular person in your life you wanted to share it with?

THE BITCH
Pilar Quintana and Lisa Dillman (Translator)

Colombia's Pacific coast, where everyday life entails warding off the brutal forces of nature. In this constant struggle, nothing is taken for granted. Damaris lives with her fisherman husband in a shack on a bluff overlooking the sea. Childless and at that age "when women dry up," as her uncle puts it, she is eager to adopt an orphaned puppy. But this act may bring more than just affection into her home. *The Bitch* is written in a prose as terse as the villagers, with storms both meteorological and emotional lurking around each corner. Beauty and dread live side by side in this poignant exploration of the many meanings of motherhood and love.

"The Bitch *is a novel of true violence. Artist that she is, Pilar Quintana uncovers wounds we didn't know we had, shows us their beauty, and then throws a handful of salt into them."* —**Yuri Herrera**, author of *Signs Preceding the End of the World*

"*A searing psychological portrait of a troubled woman contending with her instinct to nurture is at the heart of Colombian writer Quintana's slim, potent English-language debut ... The brutal scenes unfold quickly, with lean, stinging prose. Quintana's vivid novel about love, betrayal, and abandonment hits hard."* —**Publishers Weekly** (**starred review**)

"*The magic of this sparse novel is its ability to talk about many things, all of them important, while seemingly talking about something else entirely. What are those things? Violence, loneliness, resilience, cruelty. Quintana works wonders with her disillusioned, no-nonsense, powerful prose."* —**Juan Gabriel Vásquez**

ABOUT THE AUTHOR: **Pilar Quintana** is a Colombian author, who was selected by Hay Festival as one of the most promising young authors in Latin America. Her latest novel, *The Bitch*, won the prestigious Colombian Biblioteca de Narrativa Prize, and was selected for several Best Books of 2017 lists.

August 2020 | Paperback | $12.99 | 9781642860597 | World Editions

CONVERSATION STARTERS

1. How long did it take you to become fully immersed in the story?
2. Were you able to identify with Damaris?
3. Did you ever move between feeling compassion for Damaris, and judging her? If so, did you have a final conclusion on this front, and what was it?
4. Was the same true for Rogelio?
5. Is the role of family in the village recognizable? If so, how, and if not, how does it differ from what you know?
6. Do the relations of the villagers remind you of the way you relate with people in your neighborhood? If so, in which sense? If not, how do they differ?
7. Which character in the book did you relate to the most/the least? Why?
8. Does the novel have a specific message about the role of motherhood in a woman's life? Did it bring you any new ideas about this?
9. Would things have been very different if Damaris had had a child of her own?
10. Whether you live in a city or not, does the relationship the villagers have with nature differ from yours? Did you have a hard time imagining the constant struggle with animals, the jungle, and the sea?
11. Did you see the murder coming? Why? Were you horrified, or did you find the choice made sense somehow?
12. What do you think of the ending? What do you imagine will happen next?
13. To what extent is the dog's behavior Damaris's fault, or Rogelio's for that matter? What could they have done differently?
14. Do you have pets? If so, how do you think it changed the way you read this novel, if it changed it at all?
15. After finishing the book, did you feel like reading more in the same style, or from the same author?

THE BOOK OF CAROLSUE
Lynne Hugo

Brimming with wit and warmth, award-winning author Lynne Hugo's life-affirming new novel balances hardship and humor in a story about how a family gets on ... and goes on.

CarolSue and her sister, Louisa, have always been best friends, though they haven't had much in common since CarolSue married Charlie, moved to Atlanta, and swapped shoes covered with Indiana farm dust for pedicures and afternoon bridge. But when her husband dies in front of the TV while eating blueberry pie in his favorite recliner, CarolSue is left adrift and Louisa, the ever-officious retired schoolteacher, swoops in with a plan. It starts with moving CarolSue into the farmhouse she shares with a bunch of talkative chickens, a goat, puppy, and cantankerous cat.

It doesn't take long for CarolSue to remember she's not cut out for canning vegetables and feeding chickens. She resolves to ditch county life and go back to Atlanta ... until Louisa's son, Reverend Gary, arrives with an abandoned infant and a dubious story. He begs the women to look after the baby while he locates the mother—a young immigrant who fears deportation.

Keeping his own secrets, Gary enlists the aid of the sheriff, Gus, in the search. But CarolSue's bond with the baby is undeniable, and she forms an unconventional secret plan of her own ...

"Hugo deftly combines whimsy and longing, old grief and newfound joy. With her unique and compassionate voice, she writes about loss and redemption in a way that makes you laugh out loud one minute, tear up the next ... you're sure to experience tender feelings for her engaging cast of unforgettable characters." —**Diane Chamberlain,** *New York Times* **bestselling author**

ABOUT THE AUTHOR: **Lynne Hugo** is the author of ten novels, including *The Testament of Harold's Wife*. She loves hearing from readers and is available for virtual book club visits. Please visit LynneHugo.com for more information.

August 2020 | Paperback | $15.95 | 9781496725677 | Kensington Books

CONVERSATION STARTERS

1. If you have a sibling, did you have roles in your family? For example, in some families there's the smart one, the social one, the athletic one, etc. How do you see CarolSue and Louisa acting in – or sometimes breaking out of – the roles they have played in their family? Have you or a family member ever defied your own designated roles?

2. How did you react to Gary's relationship to Rosalina? Did you feel he took advantage of her? Did she take advantage of him?

3. People grieve in many ways. How would you compare and contrast CarolSue's grieving with Louisa's? If you have had or been close to a major grief experience, did either woman remind you of that? If you've not lost someone very close, do you imagine yourself reacting in one way or the other, or very differently?

4. What is your image of a woman in her late sixties or early seventies? In what ways does Louisa challenge or confirm that? What about CarolSue?

5. What do you see as the role of animals in *The Book of CarolSue*?

6. If you've read *The Testament of Harold's Wife*, how do you compare the two novels? A third book may be coming to complete a trilogy, although none will require that you have read the others. What characters from either of the first two, other than Louisa and CarolSue, would you most like to see again? Why?

7. What do you imagine as the best futures for these characters? Was the ending satisfying? What do you think will happen to Rosalina? How about Gus and Louisa? Where do you see CarolSue fitting in?

CHURCHILL'S SECRET MESSENGER
Alan Hlad

Recruited from Churchill's typing pool to become an undercover spy in German-occupied France, a young woman from London bravely endures daring missions, audacious escapes, and a harrowing imprisonment in a Nazi concentration camp, risking everything for the country – and the man – she loves.

London, 1941: In a cramped bunker in Winston Churchill's Cabinet War Rooms, civilian women huddle at desks, typing up confidential documents and reports. Since her parents were killed in a bombing raid, Rose Teasdale has spent more hours than usual in Room 60. Winning the war is the only thing that matters to her now, and she is dedicated to doing her part. When Rose's fluency in French comes to the attention of Churchill himself, it brings a rare yet dangerous opportunity ...

Rose is recruited for the Special Operations Executive, a secret British organization that conducts espionage in Nazi-occupied Europe. After weeks of grueling training, Rose parachutes into France with a new codename: Dragonfly. Posing as a cosmetics saleswoman in Paris, she ferries messages to and from the Resistance, knowing that the slightest misstep means capture or death.

Soon Rose is assigned to a mission with Lazare Aron, a Jewish French Resistance fighter who has dedicated himself to the cause with the same fervor as Rose. Yet Rose's very loyalty brings risks as she undertakes a high-stakes prison raid, and discovers how much she may have to sacrifice to justify Churchill's faith in her ...

ABOUT THE AUTHOR: **Alan Hlad** is the internationally bestselling author of *The Long Flight Home* and *Churchill's Secret Messenger*. He is also president of an executive search firm, a frequent conference speaker, and a member of the Historical Novel Society, Literary Cleveland, and the Akron Writers' Group. He lives in Ohio with his wife and children, and can be found online at AlanHlad.com.

April 2021 | Paperback | $15.95 | 9781496728418 | Kensington Books

CONVERSATION STARTERS

1. The Special Operations Executive (SOE), also known as "Churchill's Secret Army," was a real organization during WWII. Of its 470 agents in German-occupied France, 39 were women, many of whom were captured, tortured, and killed. What do you think Churchill saw in Rose that influenced him to have her recruited for the SOE? What do you think motivated Rose to join the SOE?

2. A number of historical figures make appearances in *Churchill's Secret Messenger*, including Winston Churchill and General Charles de Gaulle. Did you recognize any other characters as people who existed in real life?

3. Why do you think Rose and Muriel bonded so quickly as friends? Why is Rose determined to survive Ravensbrück Concentration Camp and deliver a message to Muriel's daughter, Mabel?

4. What makes Felix a competent SOE network organizer? What are his weaknesses as a leader?

5. While working in German-occupied France, Rose and Lazare fall in love. What brings them together? At what point do you think Rose realizes she loves Lazare? How is the war, particularly the risk of being captured by the SD, a catalyst for their affection?

6. Prior to reading the book, what did you know about the Vel' d'Hiv roundup? What could Lazare have done to save his parents?

7. Operation Jericho was a real-life RAF bombing raid on Amiens Prison, one day before over 100 French Resistance prisoners were scheduled to be executed. The name of the person who requested this actual mission remains a secret—even to this day. How likely do you think it was that a female SOE agent such as Rose was the true mastermind behind Operation Jericho? If you were Rose, would you have arranged the bombing raid, knowing that it might kill the person you love? What are the consequences of Operation Jericho?

8. How do you envision what happens after the end of the book? Do you think Rose will remain bound to her oath of secrecy? What do you think her life will be like?

CILKA'S JOURNEY
Heather Morris

Cilka is just sixteen years old when she is taken to Auschwitz-Birkenau Concentration Camp in 1942, where the commandant immediately notices how beautiful she is. Forcibly separated from the other women prisoners, Cilka learns quickly that power, even unwillingly taken, equals survival.

When the war is over and the camp is liberated, freedom is not granted to Cilka: She is charged as a collaborator for sleeping with the enemy and sent to a Siberian prison camp. But did she really have a choice? And where do the lines of morality lie for Cilka, who was sent to Auschwitz when she was still a child?

In Siberia, Cilka faces challenges both new and horribly familiar, including the unwanted attention of the guards. But when she meets a kind female doctor, Cilka is taken under her wing and begins to tend to the ill in the camp, struggling to care for them under brutal conditions.

Confronting death and terror daily, Cilka discovers a strength she never knew she had. And when she begins to tentatively form bonds and relationships in this harsh, new reality, Cilka finds that despite everything that has happened to her, there is room in her heart for love.

From child to woman, from woman to healer, *Cilka's Journey* illuminates the resilience of the human spirit—and the will we have to survive.

"[An] incredible story of bravery and love." —*Library Journal* (**starred review**)

"In the stirring follow-up to *The Tattooist of Auschwitz, Morris tells the story of a woman who survives Auschwitz, only to find herself locked away again. Morris's propulsive tale shows the goodness that can be found even inside the gulag." —**Publisher's Weekly**

ABOUT THE AUTHOR: **Heather Morris** is a native of New Zealand, now resident in Australia. In 2003, Heather was introduced to an elderly gentleman who 'might just have a story worth telling'. Their friendship grew and Lale embarked on a journey of self-scrutiny, entrusting the innermost details of his life during the Holocaust to her. Heather wrote Lale's story for her debut novel, *The Tattooist of Auschwitz*.

September 2020 | Paperback | $16.99 | 9781250265692 | St. Martin's Griffin

CONVERSATION STARTERS

1. After reading the author's note about her conversation with Lale Sokolov, the Tattooist of Auschwitz, did knowing that Cilka's story is based on a real person change your reading experience? Does the author weave fact and realistic fiction into the story effectively? In what ways?

2. What drew you to this time period and novel? What can humanity still learn from this historical space—from the front lines of an infamous concentration camp to the brutal Russian Gulags? How was this story unique in its voice and characters?

3. Is Cilka's prison sentence in Vorkuta as punishment for "sleeping with the enemy" in the concentration camp cruel? Was she forced into this role in order to survive as a mere sixteen-year-old girl? How might Cilka's outward behavior compare to her inner intentions?

4. What strategies does Cilka use to survive? Which ones does she teach the others, including Josie? How could her body be her ticket? What does she sacrifice in giving of her body but not her mind?

5. How do the women form a sisterhood or join in solidarity? Do you believe there is something universal about what they do? From snowy rescues to smuggled food—even Elena's self-inflicted burn in order to get a message to Cilka—how do the women look out for one another? How is this essential for their survival?

6. How are Cilka and Alexandr joined together? How does she administer to him and what new hope does he offer for her future? What risks? Were you surprised by their reunion on the train platform?

7. The main oppressors in this novel are men—from the commanders and guards to her fellow prisoners—and their sense of menacing entitlement and acts of rape and cruelty shape the novel. Have things changed for women in times of both war and peace when it comes to their bodies and defining their own destinies? What can society do about it?

8. Why does Cilka ultimately tell her hut-mates about her experiences and actions at Auschwitz? How does she know the time is right?

9. Why are women's voices of wartime so important to unearth and tell? What could be lost when they are unreported or underreported?

ReadingGroupChoices.com

DEAR MISS KOPP: A KOPP SISTERS NOVEL
Amy Stewart

The U.S. has finally entered World War I and Constance is chasing down suspected German saboteurs and spies for the Bureau of Investigation while Fleurette is traveling across the country entertaining troops with song and dance. Meanwhile, at an undisclosed location in France, Norma is overseeing her thwarted pigeon project for the Army Signal Corps. When Aggie, a nurse at the American field hospital, is accused of stealing essential medical supplies, the intrepid Norma is on the case to find the true culprit.

The far-flung sisters—separated for the first time in their lives—correspond with news of their days. The world has irrevocably changed—will the sisters be content to return to the New Jersey farm when the war is over?

Told through letters, *Dear Miss Kopp* weaves the stories of real life women into a rich fiction brimming with the historical detail and humor that are hallmarks of the series, proving once again that "any novel that features the Kopp Sisters is going to be a riotous, unforgettable adventure" (*Bustle*).

"Perfect for book groups." —Booklist

ABOUT THE AUTHOR: **Amy Stewart** is the *New York Times* bestselling author of the acclaimed Kopp Sisters series, which began with *Girl Waits with Gun*. Her six nonfiction books include *The Drunken Botanist* and *Wicked Plants*. She and her husband own a bookstore called Eureka Books. She lives in Portland, Oregon. For book club resources, Skype chats, and more, visit www.amystewart.com/bookclubs.

January 2021 | Paperback | $15.99 | 9780358093121 | Mariner

CONVERSATION STARTERS

1. This is the first book in the Miss Kopp series written entirely in letter form. What did you think about this structure? What did you learn about the characters through their letters that you might not have learned through a traditional format?

2. The sisters are separated for the first time in their lives and must rely on written communication. Constance is able to write at length, while at first Norma struggles to communicate, relying on her new friend Aggie to help her compose her letters. How does their writing – their styles and what they choose to share – match their personalities?

3. What surprised you about the treatment women were subjected to because of their gender during the historical period of this book, both in the U.S. and overseas?

4. In the previous Kopp Sisters books, Fleurette is extremely proud of her theatrical life and confident in her choices. But in this volume, she mentions that her contribution to the war effort – singing to the troops – is nowhere near as important as what Norma and Constance are accomplishing. How do you account for the change in her self-perception and her own value?

5. This is the first book where Norma solves a crime, without Constance to help. How do you think being separated caused the sisters to draw on one another's strengths? How did they each embody the traits of the others?

6. The sisters all mention that they can't imagine going back to the way they lived before the war. How have they been changed by the war? Why do they believe they might be discontent returning to their previous lives?

7. The ending provides a glimpse of the possibilities each Kopp sister has for her future. Are you surprised by the options available to them? What do you hope for them?

8. In the Historical Notes section at the end of the book, the author clarifies which parts of the lives of the Kopp sisters were historically known, and which she fictionalized due to a lack of information. Was the question of fact and fiction important to you while reading the novel? Does knowing this information afterward change how you think about the story?

EVERY BONE A PRAYER
Ashley Blooms

Misty's holler looks like any of the thousands of hollers that fork through the Appalachian Mountains. But Misty knows her home is different. She may be only ten, but she hears things. Even the crawdads in the creek have something to say, if you listen.

All that Misty's sister Penny wants to talk about are the strange objects that start appearing outside their trailer. The grown-ups mutter about sins and punishment, but that doesn't scare Misty. Not like the hurtful thing that's been happening to her, the hurtful thing that is becoming part of her. Ever since her neighbor William cornered her in the barn, she must figure out how to get back to the Misty she was before — the Misty who wasn't afraid to listen.

This is the story of one tough-as-nails girl whose choices are few but whose fight is boundless. Written by a survivor of sexual abuse, *Every Bone a Prayer* is a beautifully honest exploration of healing and of hope.

"Thrilling, but eerie—but it's also a painful, beautiful, and necessary examination of trauma and autonomy." —**Buzzfeed**

"Magic and heartbreak ... This is a vital story, beautifully written, and one I highly recommend." —**Kat Howard**, award-winning author of *The Unkindness of Magicians*

"Searing and soothing, honest and elusive." —**Alix E. Harrow**, author of *The Ten Thousand Doors of January*

ABOUT THE AUTHOR: **Ashley Blooms** has published short fiction in *The Year's Best Dark Fantasy & Horror*, *Fantasy & Science Fiction*, *Strange Horizons*, and *Shimmer*, and her essay 'Fire in My Bones' appeared in *The Oxford American*. Ashley is a graduate of the Clarion Writer's Workshop and the Tin House Winter Workshop and received her MFA as a John and Renee Grisham Fellow from the University of Mississippi. She was raised and lives in Kentucky. www.ashleyblooms.com

August 2020 | Paperback | $16.99 | 9781728216218 | Sourcebooks Landmark

CONVERSATION STARTERS

1. Misty's idea of inner names includes memories and sounds, things remembered and lost. What does that mean to you? Can you think of anything that would be a part of your name?

2. Compare Misty's and William's home lives. How are they each coping with the challenges of their families? Do they understand each other?

3. Misty thinks her family only notices her when she's sad or hurt. Have you ever felt like that? What did you do?

4. Why do you think Misty decides to tell her mother about Penny kissing the green glass man? Was there another choice she could have made?

5. Do you think that corporal punishment is ever justified for children? Besides the physical pain, what does Misty notice and remember about being whipped with the switch?

6. How does the environment interact with Misty's emotions? Would that relationship still exist without her empathy? How might it be different?

7. Throughout the book, Misty and Penny reach out to each other but always seem to miss. What prevents them from supporting or helping one another?

8. Misty encounters several dangers when she takes off her skin. What are they, and how does she eventually overcome them?

9. Caroline explains that she thought she could punish Earl and move on, but she might only get one of those things. What kind of justice do you think she gets in the end? Is it what she deserved?

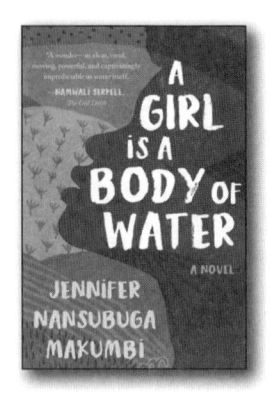

A GIRL IS A BODY OF WATER
Jennifer Nansubuga Makumbi

International-award-winning author Jennifer Nansubuga Makumbi's novel is a sweeping and powerful portrait of a young girl and her family: who they are, what history has taken from them, and—most importantly—how they find their way back to each other.

In her twelfth year, Kirabo, a young Ugandan girl, confronts a question that has haunted her childhood: who is my mother? Kirabo has been raised by women in the small village of Nattetta—but the absence of her mother follows her like a shadow. Kirabo also feels the emergence of a mysterious second self, a headstrong and confusing force inside her.

Seeking answers, she begins spending afternoons with Nsuuta, a local witch, trading stories and learning about the woman who birthed her, who she learns is alive but not ready to meet. Nsuuta also explains that Kirabo has a streak of the "first woman"—an independent, original state that has been all but lost to women.

Kirabo's journey to reconcile her rebellious origins, alongside her desire to reconnect with her mother and to honor her family, is rich in the folklore of Uganda and an arresting exploration of what it means to be a modern girl in a world that seems determined to silence women.

"A magnificent blend of Ugandan folklore and more modern notions of feminism … This book is a jewel." —*Kirkus Review* (**starred review**)

"This beautifully rendered saga is a riveting deconstruction of social perceptions of women's abilities and roles." —**Publishers Weekly**

"Jennifer Nansubuga Makumbi takes the classic male quest for identity and turns it spectacularly on its head." —**Lily King, author of** *Writers & Lovers*

ABOUT THE AUTHOR: **Jennifer Nansubuga Makumbi** is a recipient of the Windham-Campbell Prize and her first novel, *Kintu*, won the Kwani? Manuscript Project Prize and was longlisted for the Etisalat Prize. Her fiction was the global winner of the 2014 Commonwealth Short Story Prize. Jennifer lives in Manchester, UK with her husband and son.

September 2020 | Hardcover | $27.95 | 9781951142049 | Tin House Books

CONVERSATION STARTERS

1. What do the origin stories in *A Girl Is a Body of Water* tell us about the powers of storytelling or the power given to those who create foundational myths and folklore? Why do you think Jennifer Nansubuga Makumbi reclaims mythology for women in the narrative?

2. Women inform much of the action in the novel; how do they work together (or against each other) throughout the novel?

3. Uganda itself emerges as a character in the book. How did the setting and its history inform your reading of the novel? Did you consult a map at any point? Were you curious to read more about Uganda's history?

4. What role do family secrets and gossip play in this novel? Are there ways in which village gossip unearths truth, or is it always damaging?

5. Discuss the ways in which Makumbi reveals the differences in social class among her characters. What are the different cultural assumptions Kirabo encounters—the girls she meets at boarding school, the family she lives with in the city with her father, and those of the citizens in the small village of Natteta?

6. How do you think this novel would be different if it was written from Giibwa's perspective? Are there things she understands that Kirabo doesn't, and vice-versa?

7. Makumbi dedicates *A Girl Is a Body of Water* to her grandmothers, and Kirabo has many maternal figures in the novel. How is motherhood and maternal care portrayed in this novel?

8. What was it like to be immersed in Makumbi's inventive writing style and the way she weaves different languages throughout the prose? What sets *A Girl Is a Body of Water* apart from other multi-generational family sagas you have read?

9. Describe the various portrayals of marriage in the novel. What are some similarities or differences you see across generations?

10. Kirabo comes of age over the course of the novel, but she's not the only one who experiences great change. What characters change the most in your opinion?

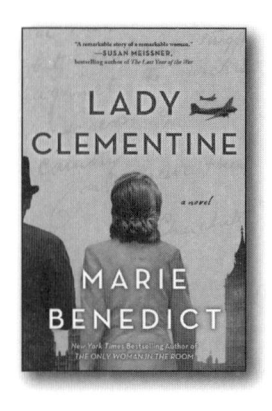

LADY CLEMENTINE
Marie Benedict

From Marie Benedict, the *New York Times* bestselling author of *The Only Woman in the Room!* An incredible novel that focuses on one of the people with the most influence during World War I and World War II: Clementine Churchill.

In 1909, Clementine steps off a train with her new husband, Winston. An angry woman emerges from the crowd to attack, shoving him in the direction of an oncoming train. Just before he stumbles, Clementine grabs him by his suit jacket. This will not be the last time Clementine Churchill will save her husband.

Lady Clementine is the ferocious story of the ambitious woman beside Winston Churchill, the story of a partner who did not flinch through the sweeping darkness of war, and who would not surrender to expectations or to enemies.

Recommended by *People*, *USA Today*, *Glamour*, *POPSUGAR*, and more!

"The atmospheric prose of Marie Benedict draws me in every single time. Compelling and immersive." —**Patti Callahan Henry**, *New York Times* bestselling author of *Becoming Mrs. Lewis*

"Benedict is a true master at weaving threads of the past into a compelling story for today." —**Susan Meissner**, bestselling author of *The Last Year of War*

ABOUT THE AUTHOR: **Marie Benedict** is a lawyer with more than ten years' experience as a litigator at two of the country's premier law firms and for Fortune 500 companies. She is a magna cum laude graduate of Boston College with a focus in history and art history and a cum laude graduate of the Boston University School of Law. She is also the author of *The Other Einstein*, *Carnegie's Maid*, and *The Only Woman in the Room*. She lives in Pittsburgh with her family.

January 2020 | Paperback | $26.99 | 9781492666905 | Sourcebooks Landmark
July 2020 | Hardcover | $16.99 | 9781492666936 | Sourcebooks Landmark

CONVERSATION STARTERS

1. Winston Churchill is one of the most recognizable figures of modern history. What did you know about his personal life before you read *Lady Clementine*? Did you have any understanding of his wife and children, and did the book challenge any preconceived ideas about his private life?

2. *Lady Clementine* opens with Clementine describing herself as being "set apart" from the rest of society. How did this feeling manifest throughout the novel, and did it change throughout her life? How did this sense of otherness impact her relationship with Winston?

3. While motherhood was different in the time period of the novel and the class in which the Churchills operated, Clementine struggled with it. How would you characterize Clementine as a mother? Did she evolve as a parent over the years? Do you feel that she crossed the line of acceptability, even in the context of her time? How did her relationship with Winston impact her mothering? Compare and contrast modern motherhood with historical motherhood from this time, keeping in mind variations in class.

4. What drew Winston and Clementine together, and how did that change over the decades? How did Winston's political alliances impact their interactions? What goal united them when their political views weren't precisely aligned?

5. After she spends time with Eleanor Roosevelt, Clementine comes to a shocking realization about Winston's view of her identity, or at least the way he presents her identity to the Roosevelts. What is the importance of female relationships in Clementine's story and in the stories of other strong women?

6. Which, if any, of the characters in *Lady Clementine* do you find yourself relating to the most? Did you connect with Clementine?

7. Winston Churchill left an enormous mark on history, and he is credited with saving Britain during World War II—but you now know that Clementine was a deeply influential figure herself. Do you think Winston would've been as successful if he didn't have Clementine supporting him? How would you characterize her legacy?

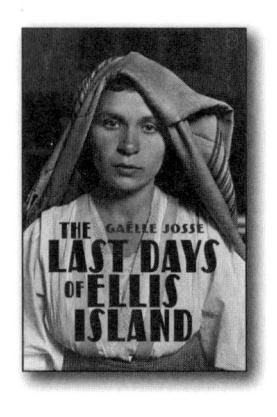

THE LAST DAYS OF ELLIS ISLAND
Gaëlle Josse and Natasha Lehrer (Translator)

Winner of the European Union Prize for Literature

New York, November 3, 1954. In a few days, the immigration inspection station on Ellis Island will close its doors forever. John Mitchell, an officer of the Bureau of Immigration, is the guardian and last resident of the island. As Mitchell looks back over forty-five years as gatekeeper to America and its promise of a better life, he recalls his brief marriage to beloved wife Liz, and is haunted by memories of a transgression involving Nella, an immigrant from Sardinia. Told in a series of poignant diary entries, this is a story of responsibility, love, fidelity, and remorse.

"*Intimate, alluring and at times haunting,* The Last Days of Ellis Island *imagines the closing hours of Ellis Island's existence as a gateway for the hopeful through the eyes of its last caretaker. Josse examines with care how life, no matter where you spend it, is a weave of wonderful moments and sad ones; moments we are insanely grateful for and moments we wish with everything within that we could take back. Eloquently and skillfully rendered.*" —**Susan Meissner**, bestselling author of *A Fall of Marigolds*

"The Last Days of Ellis Island *is a tragic story of a man who spends forty-five years working as an immigration official on Ellis island. Josse masterfully weaves this moving story of love and loss around the larger historical context of the massive wave of immigration arriving in the U.S. in the early 1900s. Beautifully written,* The Last Days of Ellis Island *is compelling historical fiction with a dash of magical realism added in.*" —**Vincent J. Cannato**, author of *American Passage: The History of Ellis Island*

ABOUT THE AUTHOR: **Gaëlle Josse** is a French poet and writer living in Paris. She received the European Union Prize for Literature for *The Last Days of Ellis Island*, along with the Grand Livre du Mois Literary Prize.

November 2020 | Paperback | $15.99 | 9781642860719 | World Editions

CONVERSATION STARTERS

1. How successful do you think Josse is in evoking the detail and atmosphere of the station at Ellis Island? Did you feel taken back to the time and place?

2. What do you think of the atmospheric and dreamy style used by Josse? How does it make you feel?

3. We see the narrator recounting his past life, but not necessarily involved in many actions in the present. What do you imagine him to spend these last days doing when he isn't writing in his diary? What sort of character do you imagine him to have?

4. Did your opinion of him change drastically throughout the course of the novel? Were you surprised at his behavior, or maybe at his reactions to his own behavior?

5. What do you think happened to Nella after leaving the station? Can you imagine her next few months, or even years? Where do you think she is now?

6. Have you or any of your family been affected by immigration/emigration? If so, how?

7. Or perhaps you even had ancestors that passed directly through the Ellis Island station itself. If so, how do you feel about Josse's fictionalization of their experience?

8. How far do you think we have come from the events narrated in the novel? Thinking about ideas such as nation-building, immigration, alienation – what do you think has changed and what has stayed the same?

9. At the end of the book, Josse gives a little bit of insight into her visit to Ellis Island; she describes her shock and "vertigo" at being in that particular place. Have you ever been overwhelmed by such a sense of "placeness," perhaps at a site of personal, national, or international history? If so, could you describe your experience?

10. What do you think Josse's intentions were in writing this novel?

11. What did you think of the ending to the story?

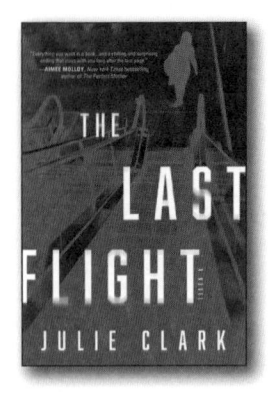

THE LAST FLIGHT
Julie Clark

Two women. Two flights. One last chance to disappear.

Claire Cook has a perfect life. Married to the scion of a political dynasty, her surroundings are elegant, her days flawlessly choreographed, and her future auspicious. But behind closed doors, that perfect husband has a temper that burns as bright as his promising political career, and he's not above using his staff to track Claire's every move, making sure she's living up to his impossible standards. But what he doesn't know is that Claire has worked for months on a plan to vanish.

A chance meeting in an airport bar brings her together with a woman whose circumstances seem equally dire. Together they make a last-minute decision to switch tickets—Claire taking Eva's flight to Oakland, and Eva traveling to Puerto Rico as Claire. But when the flight to Puerto Rico goes down, Claire realizes it's no longer a head start but a new life. Cut off, out of options, with the news of her death about to explode in the media, Claire will assume Eva's identity, and along with it, the secrets Eva fought so hard to keep hidden.

For fans of Lisa Jewell and Liv Constantine, *The Last Flight* is the story of two women—both alone, both scared—and one agonizing decision that will change the trajectory of both of their lives.

"Thoroughly absorbing." —*The New York Times Book Review*

"A page-turner!" —*People.com*

"Haunting, vulnerable ... chilling." —**Aimee Molloy**, *New York Times* **bestselling author of** *The Perfect Mother*

ABOUT THE AUTHOR: Born and raised in Santa Monica, California, **Julie Clark** grew up reading books on the beach while everyone else surfed. After attending college at University of the Pacific, she returned home to Santa Monica to teach. She now lives there with her two young sons and a golden doodle with poor impulse control.

June 2020 | Hardcover | $26.99 | 9781728215723 | Sourcebooks Landmark
May 2021 | Paperback | $16.99 | 9781728234229 | Sourcebooks Landmark

CONVERSATION STARTERS

1. What do Claire and Eva have in common? In what ways are they different?

2. How do you feel about Eva's decision to manipulate Claire?

3. Put yourself in Claire's shoes. How would it feel knowing that you've traded your life for someone else's? Would you feel guilty or fortunate? Why?

4. Describe the obstacles Claire faces once she escapes from Rory. Were there any difficulties that surprised you?

5. Compare Claire's relationships with other women in the book like Eva, Danielle, Petra, and Kelly. Are any of these women similar? In what way?

6. Discuss Eva's childhood. How does it affect how she behaves as an adult?

7. Identify some of the triggers Claire faces as a result of Rory's abuse. How do you think she can overcome them?

8. Claire makes the difficult decision to go public with her story, knowing full well that she may be met with criticism and disbelief. Why did she make this decision? Would you have handled the situation differently?

9. Liz is the only person Eva allows to get close to her. Describe their friendship. Why is it important to Eva? What does it mean to her?

10. Eva faces several huge difficulties in her life. Do you think her drug dealing is justified, given her circumstances?

11. Characterize Eva's relationship with Dex. Why does she feel betrayed when she learns the truth about him?

12. How did you feel after reading Eva's final chapter? Do you think there was anything different she could have done?

13. What do you think Claire will do next with her life? Will she be happy?

MY DARK VANESSA
Kate Elizabeth Russell

Exploring the psychological dynamics of the relationship between a precocious yet naïve teenage girl and her magnetic and manipulative teacher, a brilliant, all-consuming read that marks the explosive debut of an extraordinary new writer.

Alternating between Vanessa's present and her past, *My Dark Vanessa* juxtaposes memory and trauma with the breathless excitement of a teenage girl discovering the power her own body can wield. Thought-provoking and impossible to put down, this is a masterful portrayal of troubled adolescence and its repercussions that raises vital questions about agency, consent, complicity, and victimhood. Written with the haunting intimacy of *The Girls* and the creeping intensity of *Room*, *My Dark Vanessa* is an era-defining novel that brilliantly captures and reflects the shifting cultural mores transforming our relationships and society itself.

"Russell manages a brutal originality. ... [an] exceedingly complex, inventive, resourceful examination of harm and power." —*The New York Times Book Review*, **Editors' Choice**

"To call this book a 'conversation piece' or 'an important book' feels belittling .... [it] is so much more than that. It's a lightning rod. A brilliantly crafted novel." —*The Washington Post*

ABOUT THE AUTHOR: **Kate Elizabeth Russell** is originally from eastern Maine. She holds a PhD in creative writing from the University of Kansas and an MFA from Indiana University. She currently lives in Madison, Wisconsin. This is her first novel.

March 2020 | Hardcover | $27.99 | 9780062941503 | William Morrow
February 2021 | Paperback | $17.99 | 9780062941510 | William Morrow

CONVERSATION STARTERS

1. What is your impression of Strane? How do you interpret Vanessa's attraction to him? Do you consider him an "evil" or "sick" character?

2. At the start of her second year at The Browick School, Vanessa is lonely and withdrawn. How does this make her susceptible to Strane's advances? Do you think her seclusion contributes to the reasons Strane is drawn to her?

3. Vanessa is underage when she first has sex with Strane, but believes that she consented and wanted his attentions. Where do you see the line that separates consent and rape in this situation? If Vanessa had been eighteen at the start of their relationship, would this change your perception?

4. Discuss psychological grooming and its techniques. Do you feel you have a stronger understanding of this issue after reading the novel? What specific examples of grooming would you cite in Strane's behavior toward Vanessa?

5. Do you think that Vanessa was the first student Strane pursued in this manner? If so, why or why not?

6. Besides her seclusion, why do you think Strane singles out Vanessa? Does any of his behavior provide insights into his decision-making process?

7. Strane tells Vanessa, "It's just my luck that when I finally find my soulmate, she's fifteen years old." How do you interpret Strane expressing moral conflict over Vanessa's youth and concern for her future? Do you think he truly knows that he is doing something wrong, or is only worried about the potential consequences?

8. How do you perceive Vanessa's relationship with Jenny? Do you think things might have played out differently if Jenny hadn't started dating?

9. We move back and forth in time between Vanessa's teenage years and her present. How does Vanessa change throughout the years, or not change? What does this signify about the lasting effects of her relationship with Strane?

10. What do you think is the fundamental difference between Vanessa and Taylor and the way they respond to Strane's advances?

NOTHING TO SEE HERE
Kevin Wilson

A moving and uproarious novel about a woman who finds meaning in her life when she begins caring for two children with a remarkable ability.

Lillian and Madison were unlikely roommates and yet inseparable friends at their elite boarding school. But then Lillian had to leave the school unexpectedly in the wake of a scandal and they've barely spoken since. Until now, when Lillian gets a letter from Madison pleading for her help.

Madison's twin stepkids are moving in with her family and she wants Lillian to be their caretaker. However, there's a catch: the twins spontaneously combust when they get agitated, flames igniting from their skin in a startling but beautiful way.

Thinking of her dead-end life at home, the life that has consistently disappointed her, Lillian figures she has nothing to lose. Over the course of one humid, demanding summer, Lillian and the twins learn to trust each other—and stay cool—while also staying out of the way of Madison's buttoned-up politician husband. Surprised by her own ingenuity yet unused to the intense feelings of protectiveness she feels for them, Lillian ultimately begins to accept that she needs these strange children as much as they need her—urgently and fiercely. Couldn't this be the start of the amazing life she'd always hoped for?

With white-hot wit and a big, tender heart, Kevin Wilson has written his best book yet—a most unusual story of parental love.

ABOUT THE AUTHOR: Kevin Wilson is the author of the novels *The Family Fang*, a *New York Times* bestseller adapted into an acclaimed film starring Nicole Kidman, and *Perfect Little World*, as well as the story collections *Tunneling to the Center of the Earth*, winner of the Shirley Jackson Award, and *Baby, You're Gonna Be Mine*. He lives in Sewanee, Tennessee, with his wife and two sons.

September 2020 | Paperback | $16.99 | 9780062913494 | Ecco

CONVERSATION STARTERS

1. The twins in *Nothing to See Here* spontaneously combust when they get agitated. The fire they generate can burn others, but leaves them unharmed. What might this condition represent? Did your perception of it change throughout the book?

2. Lillian works hard to establish and maintain a bond with the twins. Why is she able to connect with them while others fail?

3. At the end of chapter three, Lillian expresses surprise that the children's hair remains unsinged after they burst into flames: "I don't know why, with these demon children bursting into flames right in front of me, their bad haircuts remaining intact was the magic that fully amazed me, but that's how it works, I think. The big thing is so ridiculous that you absorb only the smaller miracles." Do you relate to this sentiment? What other "smaller miracles" are in the story?

4. The novel offers examples of how class dynamics shape an individual's experience: Lillian and Madison's differing experiences at their elite high school, for instance, or Lillian's early days as an employee on the estate. How do wealth and privilege shape the story? Which characters most feel the impact of this?

5. How does Lillian's dark sense of humor amplify the book's themes of love, acceptance, and parenting? Did you enjoy the use of humor throughout the novel? What did it tell you about Lillian's character?

6. Lillian makes a big life change at the end of the novel. What do you think she saw in the twins that led her to make such a change?

7. Madison and Lillian have a complicated relationship that veers from deep affection to intense rivalry to bitter resentment to uneasy allies. Do you think they're foils for one another? And do you think their relationship will live on after the events of the novel?

8. *Nothing to See Here* explores different representations of family structure and dynamic. How do the family units presented at the beginning of the book evolve? What does Lillian value in family? Which characters share those values, and which characters differ?

OUR RICHES
Kaouther Adimi

Our Riches celebrates quixotic devotion and the love of books in the person of Edmond Charlot, who at the age of twenty founded Les Vraies Richesses (Our True Wealth), the famous Algerian bookstore/publishing house/lending library. He more than fulfilled its motto "by the young, for the young," discovering the twenty-four-year-old Albert Camus in 1937. His entire archive was twice destroyed by the French colonial forces, but despite financial difficulties (he was hopelessly generous) and the vicissitudes of wars and revolutions, Charlot (often compared to the legendary bookseller Sylvia Beach) carried forward Les Vraies Richesses as a cultural hub of Algiers.

Our Riches interweaves Charlot's story with that of another twenty-year-old, Ryad (dispatched in 2017 to empty the old shop and repaint it). Ryad's no booklover, but old Abdallah, the bookshop's self-appointed, nearly illiterate guardian, opens the young man's mind. Cutting brilliantly from Charlot to Ryad, from the 1930s to current times, from WWII to the bloody 1961 Free Algeria demonstrations in Paris, Adimi delicately packs a monumental history of intense political drama into her swift and poignant novel. But most of all, it's a hymn to the book and to the love of books.

"Thanks to France's 132-year colonization of Algeria, the two countries are thoroughly intertwined — a relationship Adimi explores with nuance and determination in her third novel, Our Riches, *newly translated by the excellent Chris Andrews."* —**NPR**

ABOUT THE AUTHOR: Born in 1986 in Algiers, **Kaouther Adimi** lives in Paris. *Our Riches*, her third novel, though her first to appear in English, was shortlisted for the Goncourt and won the Prix Renaudot, the Prix du Style, the Prix Beur FM Méditerranée, and the Choix Goncourt de l'Italie.

April 2020 | Paperback | $15.95 | 9780811228152 | New Directions

CONVERSATION STARTERS

1. Why did Charlot's attempt to conquer literary Paris fail?

2. What do the fortunes of secondary characters like Jean Amrouche and Mouloud Feraoun (see especially pages 109-110) tell us about the workings of power in a colonial literary space?

3. How does Adimi show the gap between Charlot's ideal of unifying the literatures of the Mediterranean and the historical realities unfolding from the 1930s to the 1960s?

4. How do Charlot, Abdallah and Ryad differ in their ways of relating to books?

5. Whose riches does the book's title refer to? And what are they?

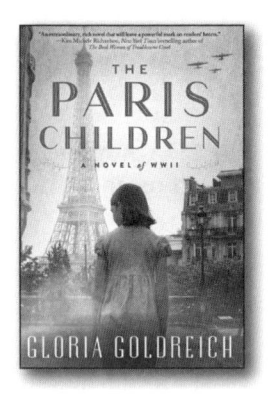

THE PARIS CHILDREN: A NOVEL OF WWII
Gloria Goldreich

Paris, 1935. A dark shadow falls over Europe as Adolf Hitler's regime gains momentum, leaving the city of Paris on the brink of occupation. Young Madeleine Levy—granddaughter of Alfred Dreyfus, a Jewish World War I hero—steps bravely into a new wave of resistance and becomes the guardian of lost children.

When Madeleine meets a small girl in a tattered coat with the hollow look of one forced to live a nightmare—a young Jewish refugee from Germany named Anna—she knows that she cannot stand idly by. Paris is full of children like Anna—frightened and starving, innocent casualties of a war barely begun. Madeleine offers them comfort and strength while working with other members of the resistance to smuggle them into safer territories. But as the Paris she loves is transformed into a theater of tension and hatred, many people are tempted to abandon the cause—and the country. And amidst the impending horror and doubt, Madeleine's relationship with Claude, a young Jewish Resistance fighter, as passionate about saving vulnerable children as she is, deepens. With a questionable future ahead of them, all Madeleine can do is continue fighting and hope that her spirit—and the nation's—won't be broken.

"Inspiring." —**Marie Benedict,** *New York Times* bestselling author of *The Only Woman in the Room*

"An extraordinary, rich novel that will leave a powerful mark on readers' hearts." —**Kim Michele Richardson,** *New York Times* bestselling author of *The Book Woman of Troublesome Creek*

ABOUT THE AUTHOR: **Gloria Goldreich** is the bestselling and critically acclaimed author of several novels, including *The Bridal Chair*. Her stories have appeared in numerous magazines, such as *McCalls*, *Redbook*, *Ms. Magazine*, and *Ladies' Home Journal*. She lives in Tuckahoe, New York.

September 2020 | Paperback | $16.99 | 9781728215624 | Sourcebooks Landmark

CONVERSATION STARTERS

1. Madeleine, with her grandfather Alfred Dreyfus as a role model, commits herself to the dangerous role of rescuing Jewish children as a Resistance fighter. What other historic or personal figures might serve as a role model to young people confronting choices that call for daring and dangerous action? Take, for example, Martin Luther King Jr., a heroic health worker, or a relative or friend whose ideals and actions you admire.

2. Given her dual roles, one as a covert Resistance fighter and the other as an agent for the Vichy government, Madeleine must often hide her true feelings. How does she accomplish this, and how might you act in similar circumstances?

3. Madeleine must balance her love for Claude against the importance of the life-saving work that engages them both. How might you confront a similar struggle in your own life? Should the needs of a larger community be prioritized rather than the yearning of an individual?

4. When Madeleine's credentials are questioned, she flirts with her interrogator. This is counter to her usual modesty, but it is a ploy that she uses to protect the children she is intent on saving. Do you think that end justifies the means? Can you think of other situations that parallel her dilemma?

5. Madeleine's physician father insists that he must treat anyone who needs his help, ally or enemy. Would you agree with his attitude?

6. Although Madeleine's primary goal is to rescue endangered Jewish children, she also becomes a demolition expert. How does she confront each role? Do they require similar skills, similar courage?

7. The Resistance demands secrecy for the protection of its members. Do you think more openness would have been helpful to their operations?

8. Resistance victories met with severe reprisals from the Nazi occupiers. How did the reprisals affect the surviving freedom fighters? Do you think that the greater good outweighs the suffering of the few?

9. Madeleine's grandmother assures her that "this life is worth its grief," an assurance that Madeleine accepts and embraces. How do you respond to that concept?

THE SOUTHERN BOOK CLUB'S GUIDE TO SLAYING VAMPIRES
Grady Hendrix

Steel Magnolias meets *Dracula* in this '90s-set, *New York Times* best-selling horror novel about a women's book club that must do battle with a mysterious newcomer to their small Southern town.

Patricia Campbell's life has never felt smaller. Her husband is a workaholic, her kids have their own lives, and she's always a step behind on her to-do list. The only thing keeping her sane is her book club, a close-knit group of women united by their love of true crime. At these meetings they're as likely to talk about the Manson family as they are about their own families.

One evening after book club, Patricia is viciously attacked by an elderly neighbor, bringing the neighbor's handsome nephew, James Harris, into her life. James is well traveled and well read, and he makes Patricia feel things she hasn't felt in years. But when children on the other side of town go missing, their deaths written off by local police, Patricia has reason to believe James Harris is more of a Bundy than a Brad Pitt. The real problem? James is a monster of a different kind—and Patricia has already invited him in.

"[A] cheeky, spot-on pick for book clubs." —*Booklist* (**starred review**)

"[O]ne of the most rollicking, addictive novels I've read in years ..." —**Danielle Trussoni** for *The New York Times Book Review*

"A delight ... its incisive social commentary and meaningful character development make [it] not just a palatable read for non-horror fans, but a winning one." —*USA Today*

ABOUT THE AUTHOR: **Grady Hendrix** is a novelist and screenwriter based in New York City. He is the Bram Stoker Award winning author of *Paperbacks from Hell*, and the Shirley Jackson and Locus Award nominated author of *Horrorstör*, *My Best Friend's Exorcism*, and *We Sold Our Souls*, which have received critical praise from such outlets as NPR, the *Washington Post*, the A.V. Club, and more.

April 2020 | Hardcover | $21.99 | 9781683691433 | Quirk Books
June 2021 | Paperback | $15.99 | 9781683692515 | Quirk Books

CONVERSATION STARTERS

1. After an uncomfortable introduction to the neighborhood, James Harris quickly and almost seamlessly transitions into being a trusted resident. Why does he fit in so well despite his sudden and surprising appearance?

2. Discuss the dynamics of the neighborhood. What are the pros and cons of living in a suburban community like Mt. Pleasant in the 1990s? Do these vary depending on gender, race, or social status?

3. The book is female-driven, and much of the horror happens to women and children. How do all the women in the book club respond to reports of strange or downright scary events, and how does their environment influence the different strengths and weaknesses they display?

4. "Something strange is going on" is a phrase Patricia repeats throughout the book. Are there red flags about James Harris early on that the women miss, or ignore? Are their reservations different from those of their husbands?

5. The response to reports of missing children in Six Mile versus Mt. Pleasant differs greatly, among both residents and law enforcement. What are the social implications of these differing reactions, and how do they influence the way the story plays out?

6. Despite the small-town charm and close-knit ties in Mt. Pleasant, Patricia finds her confidence broken again and again by people she trusts. How is her trust betrayed, both inside her social circle and beyond her community?

7. Although there is one obvious monster at the center of the story, we learn that fear, dread, and terror come in many forms. Is there more than one kind of monster? What are the scariest elements of this story and why?

8. Discuss how the women come together to end the threat to their community. Do you think the women's actions are justified, or do they go too far?

9. Discuss the novel in terms of other vampire horror fiction. What elements of vampire lore has Grady Hendrix expanded upon, discarded, and added to the genre? Do you think he has successfully furthered readers' expectations for the vampire novel?

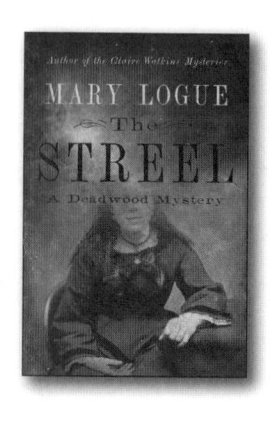

THE STREEL: A DEADWOOD MYSTERY
Mary Logue

The year is 1880, and of all the places Brigid Reardon and her brother might have dreamed of when escaping Ireland's potato famine, Deadwood, South Dakota, was not one of them. But Deadwood, in the grip of gold fever, is where Seamus lands and where Brigid joins him in an attempt to allude the unwanted attentions of the son of her rich employer in St. Paul. But the morning after her arrival, a grisly tragedy occurs; Seamus, suspected of the crime, flees, and Brigid is left to clear his name and to manage his mining claim, which suddenly looks more valuable than he and his partners supposed.

Mary Logue brings her signature brio and nerve to this story of a young Irish woman turned reluctant sleuth as she makes her way in a strange and often dangerous new world. From the famine-stricken city of Galway to the raucous hustle of boomtown Deadwood, Logue's new thriller conjures the romance and perils, and the tricky everyday realities, of a young immigrant surviving by her wits and grace in nineteenth-century America.

"Tersely and beautifully, Mary Logue recreates the muddy streets of Deadwood, the haphazard keeping of the peace, and the Black Hills gold rush of the late 1800s. The Streel *is both a taut mystery and a cautionary tale of the evils of greed. I loved the redoubtable heroine, Brigid Reardon, and I loved every stunning line of this fine story."* —**William Kent Krueger**, author of *This Tender Land*

"A well-constructed plot, lilting prose, and a heroine who's determined to escape constricting female roles make this an exceptional regional historical." —*Publishers Weekly* (**starred review**)

ABOUT THE AUTHOR: **Mary Logue** has published thirteen mysteries, nine in the Claire Watkins series, as well as poetry and young adult nonfiction and fiction, including the the bestselling *Sleep Like a Tiger*, which won a Caldecott and a Zolotow honor award.

May 2020 | Hardcover | $22.95 | 9781517908591 | University of Minnesota Press

CONVERSATION STARTERS

1. *The Streel* opens with Brigid and her brother being forced to leave their home in Ireland and emigrate to America. Was there anything in this immigration story that surprised you? Do you know when and how your ancestors came to this country? Does reading this book change how you view immigration today?

2. A title like *The Streel* brings to mind the paradox of women being either a sinner or a saint—"a virgin or a whore." If Lily is the sinner, then is Brigid the saint? In what ways are they alike? How does Logue try to humanize Lily, make her likeable?

3. When you think of your own life, what would be comparable to Brigid's immigration? Moving to a foreign country? How about being forced to colonize Mars?

4. Have you ever been to Deadwood? The Black Hills? If so, what was your impression of this area now?

5. Did you like Charlie? Was there a point at which you started to distrust him?

6. How important is it that the novel is set in Deadwood? In what ways does Logue utilize the setting?

7. Brigid is only fifteen when this novel opens. What were you like at fifteen? Can you imagine yourself, or someone you know who is this age, doing what she did?

8. The Irish at this time said short prayers throughout the day. Logue translated these prayers and had them start each section. How did these prayers work to set a tone in the book?

9. While Brigid is the main character, there are many other women in the book. Which ones stood out for you? And how were they used in the story?

10. What do you think will happen to Brigid and Padraic after they leave Deadwood? What do you *want* to happen to them?

TELEPHONE
Percival Everett

An astonishing novel about family that offers readers more than the usual possibilities

Zach Wells is a perpetually dissatisfied geologist-slash-paleobiologist. Expert in a very narrow area—the geological history of a cave in the Grand Canyon—he is a laconic man who plays chess with his daughter, trades puns with his wife while she does yoga, and dodges committee work at his college.

After a trip to the desert yields nothing more than a troubled colleague and a student with an unwelcome crush on him, Wells returns home to find his world crumbling. His daughter has lost her edge at chess, has developed mysterious eye problems, and her memory is failing. Powerless in the face of his daughter's deterioration, he finds a note asking for help tucked into the pocket of a jacket he's ordered off eBay. Desperate for someone to save, he sets off to New Mexico in secret on a quixotic rescue mission.

A deeply affecting story about loss and grief, *Telephone* offers a singular experience for reading groups, with each reader receiving one of three different texts all published under the same title.

"*Telephone*, *a novel whose multiple versions were originally intended as a secret before the coronavirus pandemic, is the latest from a rule-breaking writer.*" —*The New York Times*, "Percival Everett Has a Book or Three Coming Out"

"*Like watching a skilled juggler execute a six-ball fountain, the experience of reading* Telephone *is astonishing.*" —*Los Angeles Times*

"*God bless Percival Everett, whose dozens of idiosyncratic books demonstrate a majestic indifference to literary trends, the market or his critics.*" —*The Wall Street Journal*

ABOUT THE AUTHOR: **Percival Everett** is the author of thirty books, including *So Much Blue*, *Erasure*, and *I Am Not Sidney Poitier*. He has received the Hurston/Wright Legacy Award and the PEN Center USA Award for Fiction. He lives in Los Angeles.

May 2020 | Paperback | $16.00 | 9781644450222 | Graywolf Press

CONVERSATION STARTERS

1. What does the high specificity of Zach Wells's research focus say about him as a person? How does his research factor into the novel?

2. While reading, did you have problems distinguishing Zach Wells's dreams from his reality? How might this have impacted your understanding of the novel?

3. Do you think it was right to keep Sarah's diagnosis and consequential prognosis from her? Does Sarah ever fully realize what is happening to her? What parts of the story support your way of thinking?

4. Each section of *Telephone* is interspersed with disruptions to the narrative ("Castling Short" contains chess moves; "la grande finesse n'est pas celle qui s'aperçoit" contains descriptions of French paintings in the Louvre; etc.). How do these interludes affect the experience of the reading of the book?

5. How do racial tensions and right-wing ideologies affect the Wells family? What does *Telephone* add to the conversation surrounding racial and political tensions over the Mexican-American border? Was Zach Wells justified in being distrustful of the New Mexico police?

6. How does Zach and Meg's relationship change over the course of the novel?

7. What role does inheritance and family play in the novel? Think on the characters' bodies, lifestyles, cultural statuses, and thought patterns.

8. Why does Zach really go to New Mexico to rescue the women? How does his decision to do so relate to the other parts of his life?

9. The possibility of seeing and coming in contact with wild animals—like rattlesnakes and bears—recurs throughout the novel. Why are they important? What influence does the natural world have on those who are suffering with loss and grief?

10. Was the ending expected or unexpected? How did it differ from what you may have wanted or anticipated? How does it fit the themes of the novel?

11. Why do you think Everett titled the novel *Telephone*?

12. Did any readers in your group experience different events and even endings to the novel? If you read print editions, are there any differences on the physical books themselves?

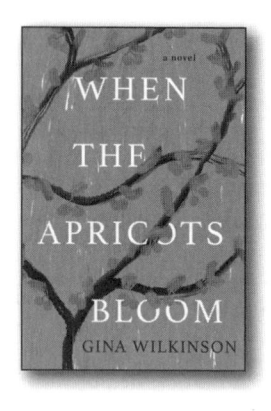

WHEN THE APRICOTS BLOOM
Gina Wilkinson

Inspired by her own experiences stationed in Baghdad during Saddam Hussein's rule, former foreign correspondent Gina Wilkinson's evocative debut is told through the eyes of three very different women in Iraq at the turn of the millennium. A secretary, an artist and a diplomat's wife each must confront the complexities of trust, friendship, and motherhood under the rule of a dictator and his ruthless secret police ...

At night, in Huda's fragrant garden, a breeze sweeps in from the desert encircling Baghdad, rustling the leaves of her apricot trees and carrying warning of visitors at her gate. Huda, a secretary at the Australian embassy, lives in fear of the mukhabarat—the secret police who watch and listen for any scrap of information that can be used against America and its allies. They have ordered her to befriend Ally Wilson, the deputy ambassador's wife. Huda has no wish to be an informant, but fears for her teenaged son, who may be forced to join a deadly militia if she refuses. Nor does she know that Ally has dangerous secrets of her own.

Also fighting to keep her child safe is Rania, Huda's former friend. As the women's lives intersect, their hidden pasts spill into the present. Facing possible betrayal at every turn, all three must trust in a fragile, newfound loyalty, even as they discover how much they are willing to sacrifice to protect their families.

ABOUT THE AUTHOR: **Gina Wilkinson** is an award-winning journalist, author, and documentarian who's reported from some of the world's most intriguing and perilous places for the BBC, NPR, and other renowned public broadcasters. During two decades living and working in hotspots across the globe, she spent more than a year in Baghdad under Saddam Hussein, at a time when Iraq was essentially sealed from the outside world. Gina now lives in Australia and can be found online at GinaWilkinson.net.

December 2020 | Paperback | $15.95 | 9781496729354 | Kensington Books

CONVERSATION STARTERS

1. *When the Apricots Bloom* was partly inspired by the author's own experiences living in Baghdad under Saddam Hussein, at a time when Western sanctions kept Iraq virtually cut off from the outside world. During that period, her closest Iraqi friend worked as a secret police informant and reported on her every move. Did her portrayal of life in Baghdad seem realistic to you? What did you learn about life for ordinary Iraqis that surprised you?

2. If you were in Huda's situation, how would you have responded to the orders from the secret police? Should Huda have felt guilty about any of her actions?

3. Compared to Huda, how does Rania handle pressure from the regime? Does her family's status protect her, or is that just an illusion? Rania is also an artist—a respected role in Iraqi society. How does this compare to prevailing attitudes toward artists in your own culture?

4. Ally is desperate to find a connection with her mother. Given the restrictions she's under, do you think her subterfuge is justified, or is her search for clues to her mother's past irresponsible? What would you have done differently?

5. Huda's husband, Abdul Amir, plays a key role in the book. To what extent does he influence Huda's decisions? Did your perception of him alter over time?

6. The novel alternates between Huda's, Rania's, and Ally's points of view. How are their worldviews and attitudes reflected in their narrative styles? Do you prefer one to the other? How would the novel have differed if it had been told from only one perspective?

7. In the acknowledgments, the author references the debate over #OwnVoices. To what extent do you agree or disagree with her statements? Do you think it was appropriate for her to write from the point of view of an Iraqi woman?

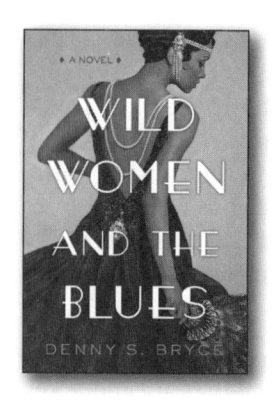

WILD WOMEN AND THE BLUES
Denny S. Bryce

Jazz Age Chicago comes to vibrant life in Denny S. Bryce's evocative novel that links the stories of an ambitious 1920's chorus girl and a modern-day film student, both coming to grips with loss, forgiveness, and the limitations—and surprises—of love.

1925: Chicago is the jazz capital of the world, and the Dreamland Café is the ritziest black-and-tan club in town. Honoree Dalcour is a sharecropper's daughter, willing to work hard and dance every night on her way to the top. Dreamland offers a path to the good life, socializing with celebrities like Louis Armstrong and filmmaker Oscar Micheaux. But Chicago is also awash in bootleg whiskey, gambling, and gangsters. And a young woman driven by ambition might risk more than she can stand to lose...

2015: Film student Sawyer Hayes arrives at the bedside of 110-year-old Honoree Dalcour, still reeling from a devastating loss that has taken him right to the brink. Sawyer has rested all his hope on this frail but formidable woman, the only living link to the legendary Oscar Micheaux. If he's right—if she can fill in the blanks in his research, perhaps he can complete his thesis and begin a new chapter in his life. But the links Honoree makes are not ones he's expecting...

ABOUT THE AUTHOR: **Denny S. Bryce** is an award-winning author and three-time RWA Golden Heart® finalist, including twice for *Wild Women and the Blues*. She also writes for NPR Books and for FROLIC Media. The former professional dancer is a public relations professional who has spent over two decades running her own marketing and publicity firm. She lives in Northern Virginia and can be found online at DennySBryce.com.

March 2021 | Paperback | $15.95 | 9781496730084 | Kensington Books

CONVERSATION STARTERS

1. When was The Jazz Age? Do you have any favorite musicians from the period?

2. Oscar Micheaux was one of several Black filmmakers who produced "Race films." These films starred Black actors and actresses who portrayed characters that weren't featured in Hollywood's racist stereotypes. How might these Race Films of the 1920s, '30s, and '40s, set the stage for the Blaxploitation films of the 1970s? (*Coffy*, *Shaft*, *Cleopatra Jones*, *Super Fly*.)

3. The music of the Jazz Age is thought to be the soundtrack of the Roaring Twenties. What music forms do you think have defined other generations?

4. Was Honoree Dalcour a "New Negro" or naturally resourceful and stubborn about what she valued about her life in Chicago?

5. How did you feel about Honoree taking in the homeless Bessie Palmer? Was it an act of kindness or frustration with the other chorus girls at Miss Hattie's Garden Cafe? Toward the end of the novel, did Honoree feel genuine affection for Bessie or more of an obligation to her pregnant roommate?

6. In 2015, Sawyer's depression was a complicated response to the loss of his sister and his estranged relationship with his father. Why do you think he is so haunted by his sister? Would he be better able to deal with his grief and guilt with a more supportive family?

7. Oscar Micheaux made more than forty films, but many were lost. In the novel, Sawyer finds a reel of film that is confirmed as a lost Micheaux. However, the most recent "find" in terms of Micheaux's lost films happened in 2017. One of Micheaux's films, *Within Our Gates*, was released in 1920 and called by some a response to D. W. Griffith's *The Birth of a Nation*, a film cited as heightening the visibility (and acceptance) of the Ku Klux Klan while promoting a negative image of African Americans. What film(s) would you credit as impacting public opinion about an individual/group or political issue? (Think about *Reefer Madness*, a 1936 film, or propaganda films of World War II, for example.)

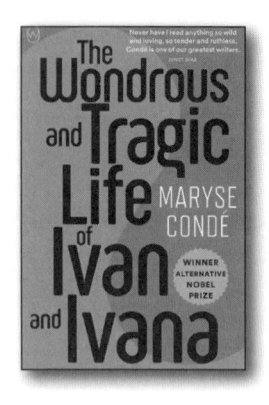

THE WONDROUS AND TRAGIC LIFE OF IVAN AND IVANA
Maryse Condé and Richard Philcox (Translator)

Born in Guadeloupe, Ivan and Ivana are twins with a bond so strong they become afraid of their feelings for one another. When their mother sends them off to live with their father in Mali they begin to grow apart, until, as young adults in Paris, Ivana's youthful altruism compels her to join the police academy, while Ivan, stunted by early experiences of rejection and exploitation, walks the path of radicalization. The twins, unable to live either with or without each other, become perpetrator and victim in a wave of violent attacks. In *The Wondrous and Tragic Life of Ivan and Ivana*, Maryse Condé, winner of the 2018 Alternative Nobel prize in literature, touches upon major contemporary issues such as racism, terrorism, political corruption, economic inequality, globalization, and migration.

"What an astounding novel. Never have I read anything so wild and loving, so tender and ruthless. Condé is one of our greatest writers, a literary sorcerer but here she has outdone even herself, summoned a storm from out of the world's troubled heart. Ivan and Ivana, in their love, in their Attic fates, mirror our species' terrible brokenness and it's improbable grace." —**Junot Díaz**

"[Condé is] at her signature best: offering complex, polyphonic and ultimately shattering stories whose provocations linger long after [the] final pages. The book is a reflection on the dangers of binary thinking … One is never on steady ground with Condé; she is not an ideologue, and hers is not the kind of liberal, safe, down-the-line morality that leaves the reader unimplicated." —**Justin Torres**, *The New York Times*

ABOUT THE AUTHOR: **Maryse Condé** was born in Guadeloupe in 1937 as the youngest of eight siblings and currently lives in the South of France. She was awarded the African Literature Prize for her worldwide bestseller *Segu* and the New Academy Prize (the "Alternative Nobel") in Literature in 2018 for her oeuvre.

May 2020 | Paperback | $16.99 | 9781642860696 | World Editions

CONVERSATION STARTERS

1. How do you interpret the reference to William Shakespeare's *Hamlet* on the very first page of the novel?

2. What role does gender play in determining the fates of Ivan and Ivana?

3. How much control do Ivan and Ivana have over their lives, and how much rests in the hands of other forces—their mother, their father, society, racism, etc?

4. What do you think of the character of the *dibia*? How does he influence the characters and plot of the novel? Do you have a sort of *dibia* in your own life?

5. What role does religion play in the forces of radicalization? What role does gender play?

6. How do you interpret the first-person plural narrator that appears throughout?

7. How does oral tradition inform the novel in terms of structure and plot?

8. On page 161, the narrator admits, "Once again we have very little reliable information as to what happened next." From where do you think the narrator has gotten this story? How many iterations of the story must there be, and what version of it do you think this is?

9. How does the presence of an unreliable narrator change the way you absorb the story?

10. What is the role of geography in the novel? How does it affect the fates of the twins? In what ways is it its own character?

NONFICTION

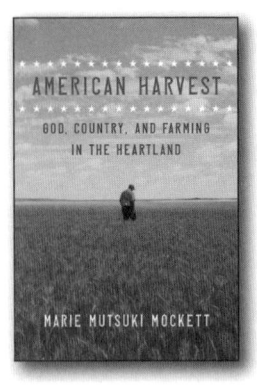

AMERICAN HARVEST: GOD, COUNTRY, AND FARMING IN THE HEARTLAND
Marie Mutsuki Mockett

For over a century, the Mockett family has owned a farm in Nebraska, where Marie Mutsuki Mockett's father was raised. Mockett, who grew up in California, with her father and her Japanese mother, knew little about farming when she inherited this land.

In *American Harvest*, Mockett accompanies a group of evangelical Christian wheat harvesters at the invitation of Eric Wolgemuth, the conservative farmer who has cut her family's fields for decades. As Mockett follows Wolgemuth's crew, they contemplate what Wolgemuth refers to as "the divide," exposing the contradictions and unhealed wounds in the American story. She joins the crew in the fields, attends church, and struggles to adapt to the rhythms of rural life, all the while continually reminded of her own status as a person who signals "not white," but who people she encounters can't quite categorize.

American Harvest is an extraordinary evocation of the land and a thoughtful exploration of ingrained beliefs. With exquisite lyricism and humanity, this astonishing book attempts to reconcile competing versions of our national story.

"*A sprawling story of pilgrimage, spiritual and personal and cultural, and Mockett's gaze is both penetrating and sweeping.*" —**The Christian Century**

"[American Harvest] *strives not only to understand the most rural parts of the heartland, but to take a good hard look at the growing divide between rural America and its urban sisters.*" —**Book Riot**

"*By turns a woman's travelogue of the Great Plains, a sweeping history of the American West, and a cross-sectional study of contemporary Christian theology.*" —**Bookforum**

ABOUT THE AUTHOR: **Marie Mutsuki Mockett** is the author of a novel, *Picking Bones from Ash*, and a memoir, *Where the Dead Pause, and the Japanese Say Goodbye*, which was a finalist for the PEN Open Book Award. She lives in San Francisco.

April 2020 | Hardcover | $28.00 | 9781644450178 | Graywolf Press

CONVERSATION STARTERS

1. Early in the book, Eric Wolgemuth identifies "the divide" in contemporary American life. What are some examples of that divide? What groups or ideas stand on either side of it? Do you agree that it's an accurate description of American society?

2. Throughout her journey, Mockett listens closely to personal experiences of faith. What are some of the different ideas she encounters about what being a "good Christian" means?

3. Mockett asks her family early in the book, "Why are our farmers and harvesters, who are conservative Christians, okay with GMOs, while people in the city, who believe in evolution, are obsessed with organic food?". (p 14) What answers does Mockett find, if any?

4. How does Mockett's experience as a woman of color play an integral part in her journey with the harvesters? Were you surprised by the direction or shape taken by her discussions about race with the people she encounters?

5. On page 52, Marie asks Juston "Did you always doubt?" In what ways are Juston and Marie similar, particularly in regards to their journeys around belief? In what ways do their approaches remain different?

6. How does Mockett's presence on the crew either create or exacerbate certain tensions? Do you think she could have done something differently? Did she succeed in bridging Eric's "divide"?

7. *American Harvest* pays close attention to the ways our preconceptions might get in the way of understanding complex realities. Did reading the book change the ways you think about any or all of the below? If so, how? • organic food • farming • the heartland • religion • urban and rural perspectives

8. Mockett spends considerable time on the road, meeting new people and engaging them in conversation. Can you think of any questions or topics you wish you could similarly explore, simply by going out and talking to new people?

9. What are some of the ways that Mockett has changed by the end of the book? What are some of the ways Eric and Juston Wolgemuth have changed?

10. How does the epigraph from Nikki Giovanni encapsulate the themes of Mockett's journey?

ReadingGroupChoices.com

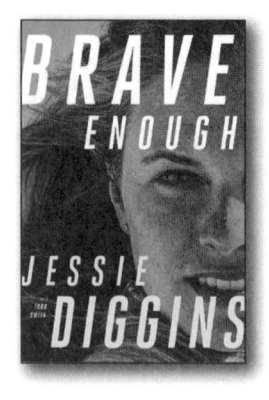

BRAVE ENOUGH
Jessie Diggins with Todd Smith

In *Brave Enough*, Jessie Diggins reveals the true story of her journey from the American Midwest into sports history, when she and teammate Kikkan Randall won the first ever cross-country skiing gold medal for the United States at the 2018 Winter Olympics. With candid charm and characteristic grit, she connects the dots from her free-spirited upbringing in Minnesota to racing in the spotlights of the Olympics. Going beyond stories of races and ribbons, she describes the challenges and frustrations of becoming a serious athlete, the intense pressure of competing at the highest levels, and her harrowing struggle with bulimia, recounting both the adversity and how she healed from it in order to bring hope and understanding to others experiencing eating disorders.

Between thrilling accounts of moments of triumph, Diggins shows the determination it takes to get there—the struggles and disappointments, the fun and the hard work, and the importance of listening to that small, fierce voice: I can do it. I am brave enough.

"With admirable vulnerability, Jessie demonstrates how to be a leader and 'best teammate' while also being open to help and support from others. I have never been more proud of my teammate and friend." —**Kikkan Randall**

"Already an inspiration to us all, Jessie once again shows her courage to leave it all on the track by sharing her deeply personal story. Readers will be encouraged by how one woman created a path forward for herself—and helped and uplifted so many in the process." —**Ann Bancroft**

"Brave Enough is a befitting title for this brutally honest and powerful book. It's an inspiring story, worthy of gold." —**Jackie Joyner-Kersee**

ABOUT THE AUTHORS: **Jessie Diggins** was raised in Afton, Minnesota, and became a professional skier at the age of nineteen. A two-time Olympian and four-time World Championship medalist, she is the most decorated U.S. cross-country athlete in World Championship history.

Todd Smith is author of *Hockey Strong*. His sportswriting has been published in *The Rake Magazine*, *Minnesota Monthly*, and *Twin Cities METRO Magazine*.

March 2020 | Hardcover | $24.95 | 9781517908195 | University of Minnesota Press

CONVERSATION STARTERS

1. "I have loved being outdoors pretty much since birth," Jessie writes to open *Brave Enough*. Diggins grew up in Afton, Minnesota, and had an extremely active childhood, surrounded by a natural world that became her imaginary kingdom. In what ways did Jessie's childhood setting inform her future career? In what ways are people a product of their environment?

2. Jessie is admittedly Type A, a personality marked by characteristics such as being goal-oriented, competitive, good under pressure, ambitious, impatient, having lots of energy, and perfectionism. Type-A students and athletes like Jessie can struggle with the desire to be "perfect" in everything they do in life. Why do you think this is? As a society, are we putting too much pressure on our high school graduates as they graduate and apply to university?

3. One of the most emotional parts of *Brave Enough* is when Jessie reveals intimate details about her eating disorder and her time in treatment at the Emily Program. In her honesty, Jessie wanted to open a conversation about eating disorders. How did these chapters affect you? What did you learn about eating disorders? How can we help others that are struggling with disordered eating?

4. Jessie has worked with a lot of amazing women and men during her career that all have different leadership styles. Kikkan Randall leads by example, Sophie Caldwell is quiet and supportive, Liz Stephen is the team Mom, and Jessie is the team's cheerleader. Which teammate's style of leadership do you most relate to?

5. In 2018, Jessie and Kikkan Randall won the gold medal in the team sprint at the PyeongChang Winter Olympics. What would it feel like to see Jessie charge toward the finish line in one of the most dramatic sprints to the finish in sports history? If you won the Olympics, what would be the first thing you'd like to do? What causes would you use your new platform for?

6. As a cross-country skier who has been traveling all around the world since her teens, Jessie has seen the effects that climate change has had on our world. For example, many World Cup races in mountain ski towns are now held entirely on artificial snow. How have you seen the changing climate impact your life or the lives of others as you travel? What actions can we all do to make a positive impact?

THE DRAGONS, THE GIANT, THE WOMEN: A MEMOIR
Wayétu Moore

An engrossing memoir of escaping the First Liberian Civil War and building a life in the United States

When Wayétu Moore turns five in Monrovia, Liberia, all she can think about is how much she misses her mother, working and studying in New York. Before she gets the reunion her father had promised her, war breaks out in Liberia, and her family is forced to flee their home, walking and hiding for weeks until they arrive in the village of Lai. Finally a rebel soldier smuggles them across the border, reuniting the family and setting them off on a journey to the United States.

Spanning this harrowing journey in Moore's early childhood, her years adjusting to life in Texas as a black woman and an immigrant, and her eventual return to Liberia, this is a deeply moving story of the search for home in the midst of upheaval. It captures both the hazy magic and stark realities of what is becoming an increasingly pervasive experience. Wayétu Moore shines a light on the great political and personal forces that continue to affect many migrants around the world, and calls us all to acknowledge the tenacious power of love and family.

"This memoir adds an essential voice to the genre of migrant literature, challenging false popular narratives that migration is optional, permanent and always results in a better life." —*The New York Times Book Review*

"An urgent narrative about the costs of survival and the strength of familial love." —*Time*

"Building to a thrumming crescendo, the pages almost fly past. Readers will be both enraptured and heartbroken." —*Publishers Weekly* **(starred review)**

ABOUT THE AUTHOR: **Wayétu Moore** is the author of *She Would Be King* and the founder of One Moore Book. She is a graduate of Howard University, Columbia University, and the University of Southern California. She lives in Brooklyn, New York.

June 2020 | Hardcover | $26.00 | 9781644450314 | Graywolf Press

CONVERSATION STARTERS

1. Who are "the dragons" and who is "the giant"? How do these imaginative elements shape and influence this nonfiction account? Who are "the women," and is it significant that they are the only non-mythical element in the title?

2. Previous accounts suggest that Liberia's Civil War erupted from ethnic tensions between descendants of resettled African Americans and indigenous groups. How does this book dispute that interpretation?

3. A passage on page 63 concerns patriarchal structures of control: "Men were talking plenty in this war. Men were deciding where to hide and what to eat and when to eat. They were deciding who would be killed and who would live." In what ways do the men in the memoir enact these dominating tendencies? Do any of them resist or embody alternative visions of masculinity, and if so, how?

4. What are some specific examples of the solidarity and care between Black women in the memoir—for instance between family members, strangers, and friends?

5. Five members of Moore's family immigrated to the United States while two were born here. How do the dynamics of being part of a mixed-status immigrant family show up in the book?

6. Compare and contrast instances in which Moore encounters explicit racism in Texas and implicit racism in New York. How do these realities affect and define Moore's understanding of the United States, both as an idea and as an actual place to live?

7. The memoir moves back and forth through time, and one section is narrated by a different voice. How do these inventive choices support and strengthen the particular story Moore has to tell?

8. When Moore returns to Liberia, she tries to find Satta, the young female rebel soldier who helped her family escape the civil war. Is Moore's quest successful? How does Satta become a central character in the narrative?

9. How does Moore resist simplistic views of trauma, both in her sessions with her therapist and in writing this narrative? What does the book demonstrate about healing?

HUDSON BAY BOUND: TWO WOMEN, ONE DOG, TWO THOUSAND MILES TO THE ARCTIC

Natalie Warren (Foreword by Ann Bancroft)

Unrelenting winds, carnivorous polar bears, snake nests, sweltering heat, and constant hunger. Paddling from Minneapolis to Hudson Bay, following the 2,000-mile route made famous by Eric Sevareid in his 1935 classic *Canoeing with the Cree*, Natalie Warren and Ann Raiho faced unexpected trials, some harrowing, some simply odd. But for the two friends—the first women to make this expedition—there was one timeless challenge: the occasional pitfalls that test character and friendship. Warren's spellbinding account retraces the women's journey from inspiration to Arctic waters, giving readers an insider view from the practicalities of planning a three-month canoe expedition to the successful accomplishment of the adventure of a lifetime.

Describing the tensions that erupt between the women (who at one point communicate with each other only by note) and the natural and human-made phenomena they encounter—from islands of trash to waterfalls and a wolf pack—Warren brings us into her experience, and we join these modern women (and their dog) as they recreate this historic trip, including the pleasures and perils, the sexism, the social and environmental implications, and the enduring wonder of the wilderness.

"Ann and Natalie would be heralded for showing that adventure can still be had in a changing environment, and that women have not only a place in the landscape of adventure, but an important voice that needs to be heard."
—**Ann Bancroft, from the Foreword**

"Hudson Bay Bound is part adventure-memoir, part nontraditional love story. Natalie Warren's adoration for the water and deep respect for the history of the land it weaves through is clear throughout the journey."
—**Gale Straub, author of *She Explores***

ABOUT THE AUTHOR: **Natalie Warren** is a Minneapolis-based author, scholar, and public speaker on environmental issues. A lifelong paddler and river lover, she canoed the length of the Mississippi River and won first place in the Yukon River Quest in the women's voyageur division, paddling 450 miles in fifty-three hours.

November 2020 | Hardcover | $24.95 | 9781517907846 | University of Minnesota Press

CONVERSATION STARTERS

1. Both Natalie and Ann had studied environmental and social issues in college. How did this trip expand their understanding of the world? What do you think they learned that they could not have fully understood by reading or talking about in a classroom setting? How might the world be different if we actually witnessed environmental and social justice issues and put more value on the lived experiences of people most impacted?

2. What did you think of the email they received from the outdoor rep before their trip? Throughout the book, the paddlers find themselves in interactions where they wonder, "Is this happening because we are women?" Have you ever experienced a situation where you were left wondering, "did that happen because of my gender, race, ethnicity, religion, or disability?" How do you work through those emotions? How can we amplify those feelings to a broader political sphere for real equitable change?

3. Ann and Natalie paddled connected waterways for nearly three months, encountering farms, dams, algal blooms, poor water quality, and pristine wilderness. What environmental lessons did they learn along the route? How do you feel about their encounters with environmental degradation?

4. Unspoken tensions build up to Ann and Natalie's epic fight on Lake Winnipeg. What did you think of their evolving friendship throughout the book? What role do fights play in "pushing the 'reset' button"? How do you handle conflict in your relationships?

5. Natalie reflects on the emotional challenges of being windbound on Lake Winnipeg. While paddling all day was hard, not being able to paddle was insurmountably more challenging. Sometimes being forced to slow down can be harder than pushing ourselves to do more and to be busier. Have you had an experience where you lost power or control to do what you wanted to do? How did you handle that situation?

6. In the afterword, Ann and Natalie reflect on the expedition, their relationship, and the impact the adventure had on their lives. What do you think about their reflection, nearly a decade after paddling to Hudson Bay? Have you ever experienced something so life-changing that you can look back and see how it changed the trajectory of your life?

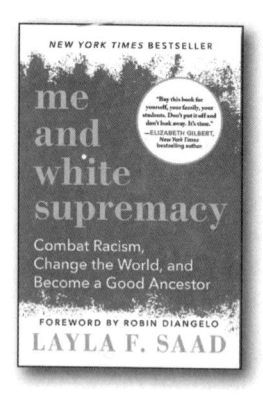

ME AND WHITE SUPREMACY: COMBAT RACISM, CHANGE THE WORLD, AND BECOME A GOOD ANCESTOR
Layla F. Saad

The *New York Times* and *USA Today* **bestseller!** This eye-opening book challenges you to do the essential work of unpacking your biases, and helps white people take action and dismantle the privilege within themselves so that you can stop (often unconsciously) inflicting damage on people of color, and in turn, help other white people do better, too.

Me and White Supremacy takes readers on a 28-day journey, complete with journal prompts, to do the necessary and vital work that can ultimately lead to improving race relations.

This book will walk you step-by-step through the work of examining:
• Your own white privilege
• What allyship really means
• Anti-blackness, racial stereotypes, and cultural appropriation
• Changing the way that you view and respond to race
• How to continue the work to create social change

"Layla Saad is one of the most important and valuable teachers we have right now on the subject of white supremacy and racial injustice." —Elizabeth Gilbert, *New York Times* **bestselling author**

"Personal, practical…effective, and imperative." —Glennon Doyle, *New York Times* **bestselling author**

"Layla Saad moves her readers from their heads into their hearts, and ultimately, into their practice. We won't end white supremacy through an intellectual understanding alone; we must put that understanding into action."
—Robin DiAngelo, *New York Times* **bestselling author of** *White Fragility*

ABOUT THE AUTHOR: **Layla F. Saad** is the author of the ground-breaking *Me and White Supremacy* and the host of Good Ancestor Podcast. She is a globally sought speaker on the topics of race, spirituality, feminism and leadership. Layla's work is driven by her powerful desire to become a 'good ancestor'; to live and work in ways that leave a legacy of healing and liberation for those who will come after she is gone.

January 2020 | Hardcover | $25.99 | 9781728209807 | Sourcebooks

CONVERSATION STARTERS

1. How will we collectively and actively continue to practice the work of antiracism and dismantling white supremacy?

2. How can we amplify and support our local, state, federal, and global BIPOC communities and organizations? What are some specific actions we can take and how will we hold ourselves accountable?

3. How can we facilitate change and inspire growth in our personal lives and systemically? Are our local and state governments actively engaged in antiracism work? If not, how can we engage them in change?

4. Is the group interested in continuing to discuss some of Layla's suggested books, podcasts, films, and/or documentaries? What would those discussions look like?

5. Would the group be interested in following up and revisiting *Me and White Supremacy* in one month, six months, or a year? How could repeating the process of reflecting on Layla's prompts be beneficial?

6. How did processing *Me and White Supremacy* as a group help and/or further our antiracism journey and confronting our relationship with white supremacy? How do we feel we have changed over the course of these group meetings?

7. How are we showing up differently for the Black and Brown people in our life? What specific actions are we taking to be present for BIPOC?

NO VISIBLE BRUISES: WHAT WE DON'T KNOW ABOUT DOMESTIC VIOLENCE CAN KILL US

Rachel Louise Snyder

Winner of the Hillman Prize for Book Journalism, The Helen Bernstein Book Award, and the Lukas Work-in-Progress Award • A *New York Times* Top 10 Books of the Year • National Book Crictics Circle Award Finalist • Los Angeles Times Book Prize Finalist • ABA Silver Gavel Award Finalist • Kirkus Prize Finalist

No Visible Bruises is the book that changed the conversation about domestic violence — an award-winning journalist's intimate investigation of the abuse that happens behind closed doors. We call it domestic violence. We call it private violence. Sometimes we call it intimate terrorism. But whatever we call it, we generally do not believe it has anything at all to do with us, despite the World Health Organization deeming it a "global epidemic." In America, domestic violence accounts for 15 percent of all violent crime, and yet it remains locked in silence, even as its tendrils reach unseen into so many of our most pressing national issues, from our economy to our education system, from mass shootings to mass incarceration to #MeToo. We still have not taken the true measure of this problem. Through the stories of victims, perpetrators, law enforcement, and reform movements from across the country, Snyder explores the real roots of private violence, its far-reaching consequences for society, and what it will take to truly address it.

"Essential, devastating reading." —**Cheryl Strayed**

"Compulsively readable ... It will save lives." —***Washington Post***

"Terrifying, courageous reportage from our internal war zone." —**Andrew Solomon**

ABOUT THE AUTHOR: **Rachel Louise Snyder** is the author of *Fugitive Denim*, *What We've Lost Is Nothing*, and *No Visible Bruises*. Her work has appeared in the *New Yorker*, the *New York Times Magazine*, the *Washington Post*, and on NPR. Snyder is an Associate Professor of Creative Writing and Journalism at American University, and in 2020–2021 she will be a Guggenheim Fellow. Follow her on Twitter at @RLSWrites.

June 2020 | Paperback | $17.00 | 9781635570984 | Bloomsbury

CONVERSATION STARTERS

1. Did the book change your mind or alter any preconceived notions you may have had about domestic violence? Which ones and how?

2. Consider Snyder's recounting of Rocky and Michelle's story. Discuss your feelings toward the friends and relatives that surrounded the couple. What is your response to their interactions with Rocky and Michelle?

3. Snyder mentions that there is no law against "psychological abuse" in the U.S.. Do you believe such a law needs to exist? Why or why not?

4. Snyder examines how domestic violence is linked to other issues like poverty, education, health care, and others. Discuss how this correlation plays out, as well as any personal experiences you may have had or observations you have made that illustrate how these issues are connected.

5. Were there any statistics or anecdotes in the book that you found particularly surprising or upsetting, or any personal stories that you found particularly moving or relatable? If so, which ones and why?

6. Snyder discusses cultural and societal norms, especially around gender, that may reinforce or even encourage the dynamics that lead to domestic violence. Do you think this is a fair assessment? Why or why not? Discuss the ways you believe societal mores do or do not contribute to a broader culture of violence and misogyny.

7. Of all the interventions and techniques Snyder investigates as possible ways to slow or halt the cycle of domestic violence, which one(s) do you think are the most crucial and why?

8. Were there any aspects of domestic violence not discussed in *No Visible Bruises* that you wish had been? If so, which?

9. Snyder writes, "Whatever we envision when we envision a victim ... none of us ever picture ourselves." Did this statement resonate with you? Do you think that is an accurate assertion? Why or why not?

10. Did the book leave you feeling hopeful or pessimistic about the future in terms of domestic violence rates and justice for the victims of domestic violence?

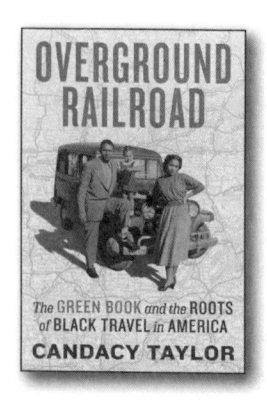

OVERGROUND RAILROAD: THE GREEN BOOK AND THE ROOTS OF BLACK TRAVEL IN AMERICA
Candacy Taylor

Published from 1936 to 1966, the *Green Book* was hailed as the "black travel guide to America." At that time, it was very dangerous and difficult for African Americans to travel because black travelers couldn't eat, sleep, or buy gas at most white-owned businesses. The *Green Book* listed hotels, restaurants, gas stations, and other businesses that were safe for black travelers. It was a resourceful and innovative solution to a horrific problem. It took courage to be listed in the *Green Book,* and *Overground Railroad* celebrates the stories of those who put their names in the book and stood up against segregation. It shows the history of the *Green Book*, how we arrived at our present historical moment, and how far we still have to go when it comes to race relations in America.

"A fascinating history of black travel . . . telling the sweeping story of black travel within Jim Crow America across four decades." — **The New York Times Book Review**

"In scope and tone, Overground Railroad *recalls Isabel Wilkerson's* The Warmth of Other Suns ... *At its center, the book is a nuanced commentary of how black bodies have been monitored, censured or violated, and it compellingly pulls readers into the current news cycle." —***The Los Angeles Times**

ABOUT THE AUTHOR: **Candacy Taylor** is an award-winning author, photographer and cultural documentarian. Her work has been featured in over 50 media outlets including the *New Yorker*, *The Atlantic*, and *Newsweek*. She is the recipient of numerous fellowships and grant awards including The Hutchins Center at Harvard University, The Schomburg Center, The National Endowment for the Humanities, The National Park Service, The American Council of Learned Societies, and National Geographic. She received an Archie Green Fellowship from the American Folklife Center at the Library of Congress, and was the only person to have received the award twice. She lives in Denver, Colorado.

January 2020 | Hardcover | $35.00 | 9781419738173 | Abrams Press

CONVERSATION STARTERS

1. Throughout the book, what were the most common images or stories you associated with "driving while black"? How does the author's description align with or differ from those images or stories?

2. Discuss the book's title and how the dangers on the modern roads of the *Green Book* era (circa 1934–1970) were the same or different from the Underground Railroad during the slavery era.

3. The author presents *Green Book* publisher, Victor Hugo Green, in heroic terms, stating that the guide's longevity and success stem from his "vision, grit, creativity, and stamina." Was he a hero? Should he be regarded as important a publisher as John H. Johnson of *Ebony* and *Jet* magazines?

4. Why do you think the *Green Book* lasted for decades, outlasting all of the other travel guides for African American people?

5. The author states that "given the violence that black travelers encountered on the road, the *Green Book* was an ingenious solution to a horrific problem." What other solutions could have been possible?

6. Of the many sites mentioned from the Jim Crow era, very few of them are still in existence. On the subject of integration, Florida activist Georgia Ayers states, "We got what we wanted, but we lost what we had." Do you agree or disagree? Why?

7. The author helps readers make connections between white supremacy and government policies that impacted the lives of Black people. How have times changed or remained the same?

8. In what ways are current travel restrictions to African American people similar to those that are represented in the book? In addition to the dangers of "driving while black" and being stopped by the police, what other kinds of discrimination did Black people experience? How are these discriminatory practices still evident in today's society?

9. Why do you think the author used her stepfather's experiences to relay the dangers of travel for African American people? How did his life experiences parallel the broader historic experiences that Taylor discusses throughout the book?

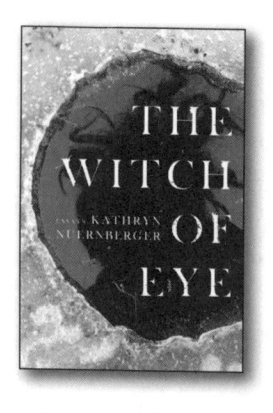

THE WITCH OF EYE: ESSAYS
Kathryn Nuernberger

This amazingly wise and nimble collection investigates the horrors inflicted on so-called "witches" of the past. *The Witch of Eye* unearths salves, potions, and spells meant to heal, yet interpreted by inquisitors as evidence of evil. The author describes torture and forced confessions alongside accounts of gentleness of legendary midwives. In one essay about a trial, we learn through folklore that Jesus's mother was a midwife who cured her own son's rheumatism. In other essays there are subtle parallels to contemporary discourse around abortion and environmental destruction. Nuernberger weaves in her own experiences, too. There's an ironic look at her own wedding, an uncomfortable visit to the Prague Museum of Torture, and an afternoon spent tearing out a garden in a mercurial fit. Her researched material is eye-opening, lively, and often funny. An absolutely thrilling collection.

"A magnificent book, full of incidental pleasures, and incidental terrors, and fundamental truths. Nuernberger writes like a Baudelaire who instead of walking across a city can walk across time." —**Rivka Galchen, author of** *Little Labors*

"Seething with the historical, the scholarly, and the personal, *The Witch of Eye* is an igneous cauldron for the witchiest of intellectuals and revolutionaries." —**Sharma Shields, author of** *The Cassandra*

ABOUT THE AUTHOR: **Kathryn Nuernberger** is the author of three poetry collections, *Rue*, *The End of Pink*, and *Rag & Bone*, as well as the essay collection *Brief Interviews with the Romantic Past*. A recipient of grants and fellowships from the NEA, H. J. Andrews Experimental Forest, Bakken Museum of Electricity in Life, and American Antiquarian Society, she was awarded the James Laughlin Prize from the Academy of American Poets and has twice been included on the list of *Best American Notable Essays*. She teaches on the faculty of the MFA program at the University of Minnesota.

February 2021 | Paperback | $16.95 | 9781946448705 | Sarabande Books

CONVERSATION STARTERS

1. With which witch in this book do you identify most closely or personally?

2. Of all the spells described in this book, which one would you most like to try yourself?

3. How are the historical figures in this book similar to or different from your earlier ideas about who witches were?

4. Michel de Certeau has said that the key question of a historian is to discover what makes ideas become thinkable. What factors do you think make witch trials thinkable in different times and places throughout history?

5. In many accounts of the Salem witch trials, Titiba is blamed for the craze that overtook the village. Why do you think there has been such a rush to scapegoat her in this way and what factors do you think contributed to this defining moment in American history?

6. Most accused witches eventually confessed, under pain or threat of torture. Why was it so important to the inquisitors to hear that testimony and why was it so significant when women like Lisbet Nypan, Titiba, and Maria Barbosa withheld such confessions?

7. There are many similarities between Hildegaard von Bingen and Angela de la Barthe. Why was the former canonized as a saint while the latter was executed for witchcraft?

8. There is a fair amount of overlap between the history of witch trials and the history of midwifery. What socio-historical forces and ideologies have caused suspicions of malfeasance to be attached to the profession of midwifery?

9. The historian Laura de Mello e Souza has written that through a subaltern mode of historiography, "it becomes possible to make out faces in the crowd, to extend the historical concept of 'individual' in the direction of lower classes." What are the challenges in telling the stories of accused witches with historical accuracy?

10. Which of the accused witches do you most want to know more about?

WOMEN ROWING NORTH: NAVIGATING LIFE'S CURRENTS AND FLOURISHING AS WE AGE
Mary Pipher

From Mary Pipher, the *New York Times* bestselling author of *Reviving Ophelia*, *Women Rowing North* is a guide to wisdom, authenticity, and bliss for women as they age.

Women growing older contend with ageism, misogyny, and loss. Yet as Mary Pipher shows, most older women are deeply happy and filled with gratitude for the gifts of life. Their struggles help them grow into the authentic, empathetic, and wise people they have always wanted to be.

In *Women Rowing North*, Pipher offers a timely examination of the cultural and developmental issues women face as they age. Drawing on her own experience as daughter, sister, mother, grandmother, caregiver, clinical psychologist, and cultural anthropologist, she explores ways women can cultivate resilient responses to the challenges they face. "If we can keep our wits about us, think clearly, and manage our emotions skillfully," Pipher writes, "we will experience a joyous time of our lives. If we have planned carefully and packed properly, if we have good maps and guides, the journey can be transcendent."

"Thoughtful, wise, and profoundly transformative ... This is truly a one-of-a-kind book, one that I've been waiting for." —**Julia Alvarez, author of** *How the Garcia Girls Lost Their Accents* **and** *Once Upon A Quinceanera: Coming of Age in the USA*

"An enlightening look at how women can age joyfully." —*People*

ABOUT THE AUTHOR: **Mary Pipher** is a psychologist specializing in women, trauma, and the effects of our culture on mental health, which has earned her the title of "cultural therapist" for her generation. She is the author of several *New York Times* bestsellers, including *Reviving Ophelia*, *The Shelter of Each Other*, and *Another Country*. She lives in Lincoln, Nebraska.

March 2020 | Paperback | $17.00 | 9781632869616 | Bloomsbury

CONVERSATION STARTERS

1. This book explores the reality of a specific stage of women's lives as opposed to the dominant cultural stories about us. Pipher writes: "What women mean when they say, 'I am not old,' is, 'I won't accept the ideas that the culture has about me.'" (p 27) How do Pipher's stories about women she's met differ from the cultural stereotypes you've encountered?

2. Pipher, known for her *New York Times* bestseller *Reviving Ophelia* about the experience of teenage girls, exhibits her compassion while addressing the unique issues of her own age group. "When I told my adolescent granddaughter Kate about this book, I stressed that every life stage is hard. Looking back across my life decade by decade, I cannot find one that is without anguish." (p 18) Do you share a compassion with younger generations, or do you feel that some stages of life are more difficult than others?

3. Pipher explores ways women can cultivate resilient responses to the challenges they face, both internal and interpersonal. What resilient foundations have you built in your life, and what would you like to build?

4. Pipher distinguishes between having a "happy" life and having a "meaningful" life, quoting Emily Esfahani-Smith: "Happiness seekers are unhappy when they don't get what they want. Meaning seekers can survive negative events." (p 63) How do you think people can center their lives on finding meaning rather than happiness?

5. Pipher writes about forming your own narrative about your life: "Even our most painful experiences can be revisited. We can ask, 'How did that make me stronger?' 'What did I learn from that experience?' 'What am I proud of when I look back on that day?'" (p 149) Much of this book is about reclaiming the collective narrative about aging. How is Pipher reframing that understanding? What are other questions people can ask to reassess their own stories?

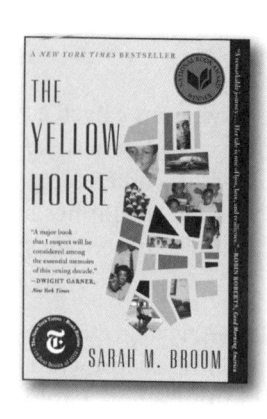

THE YELLOW HOUSE: A MEMOIR
Sarah M. Broom

Winner of the 2019 National Book Award in Nonfiction, *The Yellow House* is a brilliant, haunting and unforgettable memoir from a stunning new talent about the inexorable pull of home and family, set in a shotgun house in New Orleans East.

A book of great ambition, Sarah M. Broom's memoir tells a hundred years of her family and their relationship to home in a neglected area of one of America's most mythologized cities. This is the story of a mother's struggle against a house's entropy, and that of a prodigal daughter who left home only to reckon with the pull that home exerts, even after the Yellow House was wiped off the map after Hurricane Katrina. *The Yellow House* expands the map of New Orleans to include the stories of its lesser known natives, demonstrating how enduring drives of clan, pride, and familial love resist and defy erasure.

"A major book that I suspect will come to be considered among the essential memoirs of this vexing decade." —**New York Times**

"Gorgeous ... reads as elegy and prayer ... Sarah M. Broom is a writer of great intellect and breadth." —**NPR**

"A remarkable journey ... Her tale is one of loss, love, and resilience." —**Robin Roberts, Good Morning America**

"An extraordinary, engrossing debut ... [Broom] pushes past the baseline expectations of memoir as a genre to create an entertaining and inventive amalgamation of literary forms." —**New York Times Book Review**

ABOUT THE AUTHOR: **Sarah M. Broom** is a writer whose work has appeared in the *New Yorker*, *The New York Times Magazine*, *The Oxford American*, and *O, The Oprah Magazine* among others. She was awarded a Whiting Foundation Creative Nonfiction Grant in 2016 and was a finalist for the New York Foundation for the Arts Fellowship in Creative Nonfiction in 2011. She has also been awarded fellowships at Djerassi Resident Artists Program and The MacDowell Colony. She lives in New York.

June 2020 | Paperback | $17.00 | 9780802149039 | Grove Atlantic

CONVERSATION STARTERS

On perspective:
1. At the opening of the story, Sarah Broom describes the lot where the Yellow House once stood from fifteen thousand feet above, saying that from those great heights, her brother Carl, who tends the space, would not be seen.
2. Have you ever brought up a Google Earth image of your house from above and zoomed out? What impact did seeing your home, your street, your state, your country shrink in comparison to the world have on your perspective?

On names:
1. The author refers to Hurricane Katrina throughout as "the Water."
2. Why do you think she made this choice? Describe what "the Water" communicates to you, and how it changed over the course of the book. Do you think it will be the same for every reader?

On family firsts:
1. On page 57, Broom writes: "Mom paid for her house with money from Webb's life insurance policy. She was nineteen years old, the first in her immediate family to own a house, a dream toward which her own mother, Lolo, still bent all of her strivings."
2. Who accomplished these kinds of firsts in your family? Were they long-ago accomplishments or more recent? What kinds of sacrifices or good-willed pitching in were made and by whom to help make them possible?

On the growing-up world:
1. In the chapter "Map of My World," the author describes five points on the map that make "my growing-up world." (p 117)
2. What are some of the places that you can still inhabit vividly in your mind's eye? Why do you think those stuck and not others? Why do you think the points in the author's growing-up world stuck with her so strongly?

On the long-term impact of catastrophe:
1. During the Water, Broom writes, "All told, we scatter in three cardinal directions, nine runny spots on the map." Even after it recedes, most remain dispersed. How do climate events like the hurricane impact families, employment, housing prices? What effect do you think this kind of scattering after climate crises has on regional culture?

YOUNG ADULT

ALL THIRTEEN: THE INCREDIBLE CAVE RESCUE OF THE THAI BOYS' SOCCER TEAM
Christina Soontornvat

A unique account of the amazing Thai cave rescue told in a heart-racing, you-are-there style that blends suspense, science, and cultural insight.

On June 23, 2018, twelve young players of the Wild Boars soccer team and their coach enter a cave in northern Thailand seeking an afternoon's adventure. But when they turn to leave, rising floodwaters block their path out. The boys are trapped. Before long, news of the missing team spreads, launching a seventeen-day rescue operation involving thousands of rescuers from around the globe. As the world sits vigil, people begin to wonder: how long can a group of ordinary kids survive in complete darkness, with no food or clean water? Luckily, the Wild Boars are a very extraordinary "ordinary" group. Combining firsthand interviews of rescue workers with in-depth science and details of the region's culture and religion, author Christina Soontornvat—who was visiting family in Northern Thailand when the Wild Boars went missing—masterfully shows how both the complex engineering operation above ground and the mental struggles of the thirteen young people below proved critical in the life-or-death mission.

Meticulously researched and generously illustrated with photographs, this page-turner includes an author's note describing her experience meeting the team, detailed source notes, and a bibliography to fully immerse readers in the most ambitious cave rescue in history.

"An extraordinary story, marvelously told." —**Martin W. Sandler, National Book Award Winner**

"The term page-turner gets tossed around a lot, but All Thirteen *is the real deal. Even if you think you know this story, you won't be able to stop reading."* —**Steve Sheinkin, award-winning author of** *Bomb* **and** *Undefeated*

"A nonfiction marvel." —**Minh Lê, award-winning author of** *Drawn Together*

ABOUT THE AUTHOR: **Christina Soontornvat** is the author of several books for young readers. She holds a bachelor's in mechanical engineering and a master's in science education. Christina Soontornvat lives with her family in Austin, Texas.

October 2020 | Hardcover | $24.99 | 9781536209457 | Candlewick Press

CONVERSATION STARTERS

1. What is your impression of the boys as a group? How do they interact with each other and with their coach? Does the time in the cave change their relationships? Describe a few of those trapped in the cave and how the author conveys their personalities.

2. Why did Coach Ek and the boys have reason to believe it would be safe to visit the cave? What unexpected forces of nature worked against them? What role might climate change have played in this? Explain geographical features and aspects of weather that made the rescue difficult. What made their days in the cave dangerous?

3. Different groups involved in the rescue had different opinions about how it should be done. At one point, the author writes, "Relationships between the diving team and the Thai authorities become tense." (p 99) What are the different opinions? How is conflict resolved at this point and other times during the rescue?

4. Cultural differences crop up at various times in the rescue. In the situation in the previous question, the Thai military considered the divers rude. Later in the cave, the divers "seem stunned that the kids are so upbeat." (p 140) Discuss these and other cultural differences. How would understanding each other's culture help in these situations?

5. Why was there resistance to a dive rescue? What were the other possible rescue solutions, and what were the problems with each alternative?

6. Even if you know before reading the book that the boys survived, the narrative is suspenseful. What is innately dramatic about the story? What emotions does it raise in you as a reader? What narrative techniques does the author use to intensify the suspense?

7. The author draws readers into the story through imagery and figurative language. She also uses words related to the senses to make scenes come alive. Find examples of these narrative devices and discuss their impact. Also discuss the use of the present tense and its effect on the narrative.

8. How do the visual aspects of the book help convey information, personalities, and emotions? How do the maps and diagrams make the rescue operation easier to understand? Discuss the use of sidebars and what they add to your understanding of technical topics and of Thai culture.

BLACK BROTHER, BLACK BROTHER
Jewell Parker Rhodes

From award-winning and bestselling author Jewell Parker Rhodes comes a powerful coming-of-age story about two brothers, one who presents as white, the other as black, and the complex ways in which they are forced to navigate the world, all while training for a fencing competition.

Sometimes, 12-year-old Donte wishes he were invisible. As one of the few black boys at Middlefield Prep, most of the students don't look like him. They don't like him either. Dubbing him "Black Brother," Donte's teachers and classmates make it clear they wish he were more like his lighter-skinned brother, Trey.

When he's bullied and framed by the captain of the fencing team, "King" Alan, he's suspended from school and arrested for something he didn't do.

Terrified, searching for a place where he belongs, Donte joins a local youth center and meets former Olympic fencer Arden Jones. With Arden's help, he begins training as a competitive fencer, setting his sights on taking down the fencing team captain, no matter what.

As Donte hones his fencing skills and grows closer to achieving his goal, he learns the fight for justice is far from over. Now Donte must confront his bullies, racism, and the corrupt systems of power that led to his arrest.

Powerful and emotionally gripping, *Black Brother, Black Brother* is a careful examination of the school-to-prison pipeline and follows one boy's fight against racism and his empowering path to finding his voice.

"A powerful work." —*Booklist* (**starred review**)

"Celebrates finding one's place in the world." —*School Library Connection* (**starred review**)

ABOUT THE AUTHOR: **Jewell Parker Rhodes** is the author of *Ninth Ward*, winner of a Coretta Scott King Honor, *Sugar*, winner of the Jane Addams Children's Book Award, and the *New York Times*-bestselling *Ghost Boys*. She has also written many award-winning novels for adults. When she's not writing, Jewell visits schools to talk about her books and teaches writing at Arizona State University.

March 2020 | Hardcover | $16.99 | 9780316493802 |
Little, Brown Books for Young Readers

CONVERSATION STARTERS

1. Donte and Trey have a strong brotherly bond. How do they make space for one another? How do they include each other?

2. How do Donte and Trey's friends support them? What specific actions do they take to make Donte and Trey feel safer and more included at school? What do you think it means to be an ally?

3. How do people react to Trey and his dad compared to Donte and his mom?

4. Fencing is described as an elite sport. What barriers make fencing difficult for more people to get involved in?

5. Coach eventually reveals his personal history with fencing to Donte. How do these revelations about Coach's past affect Donte's decisions in the present? How does Donte benefit from having Coach as a role model?

6. How does Donte change as he learns to fence? In what ways does he begin to think differently?

7. Donte remarks that he's "got to be careful" walking around his neighborhood. (p 33) Why does Donte think this? How does this awareness affect his interactions with authority figures like his headmaster and the police?

8. The Middlefield Prep school motto is *non nobis solum*, which the headmaster translates as "not for ourselves alone". (p 194) Do you think Middlefield lives up to this motto? How so?

9. Zarra tells Donte about the Alexandre Dumas biography *The Black Count*. How do the stories we are told impact how we view the world? Does history always show us the full story?

10. Through training, Donte discovers that fencing is a sport based on rules and etiquette. How can you apply the rules of fencing, namely "courage, honor, integrity, and chivalry," to your everyday life? (p 189)

THE BURNING
Laura Bates

An Amazon Best Book of the Month!

A rumor is like fire. And a fire that spreads online ... is impossible to extinguish.

New school. Check.

New town. Check.

New last name. Check.

Social media profiles? Deleted.

Anna and her mother have moved hundreds of miles to put the past behind them. Anna hopes to make a fresh start and escape the harassment she's been subjected to. But then rumors and whispers start, and Anna tries to ignore what is happening by immersing herself in learning about Maggie, a local woman accused of witchcraft in the seventeenth century. A woman who was shamed. Silenced. And whose story has unsettling parallels to Anna's own.

From Laura Bates, internationally renowned feminist and founder of the Everyday Sexism Project, comes a realistic fiction story for the #metoo era. It's a powerful call to action, reminding all readers of the implications of sexism and the role we can each play in ending it.

"A smart, explosive examination of gender discrimination and its ramifications." —***Publishers Weekly***

"Emotionally charged ... powerful." —***Booklist***

ABOUT THE AUTHOR: Laura Bates is a UK-based author and the founder of the Everyday Sexism Project—a crowd-sourced collection of stories from women around the world about their experiences with gender inequality. Laura received the 2015 British Empire Medal in the Queen's Birthday Honours, was named in the BBC Woman's Hour Power List 2014 Game Changers, and has won *Cosmopolitan*'s Ultimate Woman of the Year Award. She was also named to CNN's 10 Visionary Women List. Follow her efforts on Twitter @everydaysexism.

April 2020 | Hardcover | $17.99 | 9781728206738 | Sourcebooks Fire

CONVERSATION STARTERS

1. Maggie's story, though four hundred years old, has been handed down for centuries through local accounts and area folklore. And Anna's story is based on real-life experiences of thousands of teenage girls. What are the main similarities and differences in their stories?

2. Have things changed dramatically for young women in those four hundred years?

3. How do you feel about the conversation between Anna and Emily Winters? How do you think both girls feel afterward?

4. How well do you think Ms. Forsyth and Miss Evans handle the information they learn about Anna online? Is there anything they could have done differently to better support her?

5. When Robin tries to stand up for Anna, he experiences homophobic bullying from some other boys. What pressures do the young men in the novel face, from one another, and from the outside?

6. What do you think Anna's mother is thinking and feeling when they arrive in St. Monans?

7. How would you describe Anna's relationship with her mother? Does it change over the course of the novel?

8. Why do you think Headmaster Greaves reacts the way he does to Anna's situation?

9. How would you describe Alisha's character? What do you think about the way she defines true love in her conversation with Anna on the pier?

10. Alisha and Cat are very different but are extremely close friends. What do you think makes their relationship so strong?

11. How do you think Anna's old friends back in Birmingham feel now that she is gone? Do you think the way they feel about Anna will change as they grow older?

12. Both Anna and Cat experience backlash for making decisions about their own bodies. In what ways are girls' bodies policed in the novel and in real life?

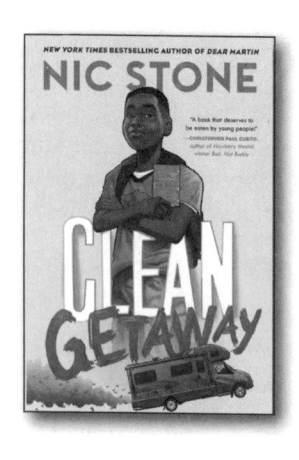

CLEAN GETAWAY
Nic Stone

How to Go on an Unplanned Road Trip with Your Grandma:

Grab a Suitcase: Prepacked from the big spring break trip that got CANCELLED.

Fasten Your Seatbelt: G'ma's never conventional, so this trip won't be either.

Use the *Green Book*: G'ma's most treasured possession. It holds history, memories, and most important, the way home.

What Not to Bring:

A Cell Phone: Avoid contact with Dad at all costs. Even when G'ma starts acting stranger than usual.

Take a trip through the American South with the *New York Times* bestselling author Nic Stone and an eleven-year-old boy who is about to discover that the world hasn't always been a welcoming place for kids like him, and things aren't always what they seem—his G'ma included.

"A road novel that serves in part as a primer on important scenes and themes of the civil-rights movement ... [A] poignant caper." —*The Wall Street Journal*

ABOUT THE AUTHOR: **Nic Stone** is an Atlanta native and a Spelman College graduate. After working extensively in teen mentoring and living in Israel for several years, she returned to the United States to write full-time. Nic's debut novel for young adults, *Dear Martin*, was a *New York Times* bestseller and a William C. Morris Award finalist. She is also the author of *Odd One Out*, *Jackpot*, and *Dear Justyce*.

January 2020 | Hardcover | $16.99 | 9781984892973 |
Crown BFYR from Random House Children's Books

CONVERSATION STARTERS

1. What is your initial impression of Scoob? Why do you feel this way? What is your initial impression of G'ma? Why?

2. Scoob says that the RV gives him "the willies". (p 9) Why does Scoob feel this way? He misses G'ma's house. Why do we become attached to places? Is it really about the place?

3. Scoob is in trouble with his father. Why? What happened at school? What do you think Scoob's father means when he says, "the punishment is harsher and the fallout is infinitely worse"? Who are "boys like you"? (p 13-17)

4. Who is Shenice? Who is Drake? What is epilepsy? What do you think about how Scoob responded to Bryce bullying Drake?

5. Why was *The Travelers' Green Book* a necessary brochure when G'ma and G'pop were young adults?

6. Why do you suppose G'ma is swapping the license plates on the RV? (p 43-44)

7. G'ma keeps calling Scoob, "Jimmy". Why? Who is Jimmy? What do you think is happening to G'ma? (p 82-83)

8. Scoob believes G'ma is being less than truthful with him because she starts to whistle. How do you know if someone is being dishonest with you? What can you do about it?

9. G'ma is overwhelmed with guilt. Why does she think that being pulled over with G'pop was her fault? (p 135-136)

10. Chapter 15 details Scoob's dream about being back at home with his dad. What do you think this dream means?

11. Why do you think Scoob's mom is out of his and his father's lives? Why do you think Scoob is not ready to reconnect with her? (p 216)

12. What does Scoob find inside G'ma's treasure chest? What do its contents inspire Scoob and his dad to do?

FIREKEEPER'S DAUGHTER
Angeline Boulley

Keep the secret. Live the lie. Earn your truth.

Angeline Boulley's *Firekeeper's Daughter* is a groundbreaking thriller about a Native teen who goes undercover to root out the crime and corruption threatening her community.

Eighteen-year-old Daunis Fontaine wants to leave home to discover who she really is. As a biracial science geek and hockey star, she's always felt like an outsider, both in her hometown and on the nearby Ojibwe reservation. But when her family is struck by tragedy, Daunis puts her dreams on hold to care for her fragile mother. The only bright spot is meeting Jamie, the charming new recruit on her brother's hockey team.

Then Daunis witnesses a shocking murder, thrusting her into the heart of an ongoing FBI investigation. As an undercover informant, Daunis works tirelessly to expose the criminals. But as the secrets pile up and the deception strikes close to home, Daunis must learn what it means to be a strong Anishinaabe kwe (Ojibwe woman).

ABOUT THE AUTHOR: **Angeline Boulley**, an enrolled member of the Sault Ste. Marie Tribe of Chippewa Indians, is a storyteller who writes about her Ojibwe community in Michigan's Upper Peninsula. She was selected as an emerging Young Adult writer in the 2019 We Need Diverse Books Mentorship Program and chosen to attend the 2019 Tin House YA Writers Workshop. As a former Director of the Office of Indian Education at the U.S. Department of Education, she focused on improving the education of Native American students at the tribal, state, regional, and national levels. She lives and works in the Washington, D.C. area, but her home will always be on Sugar Island. *Firekeeper's Daughter* is her debut novel. Visit angelineboulley.com.

March 2021 | Hardcover | $18.99 | 9781250766564 |
Henry Holt and Co. (BYR) An imprint of Macmillan

CONVERSATION STARTERS

1. Daunis starts every day with a prayer and a morning run. What is the significance of ritual to Daunis? What other rituals does she engage in?

2. Daunis talks about keeping her various "worlds" separate, saying, "My life goes more smoothly when Hockey World and Real World don't overlap. Same as with my Fontaine and Firekeeper worlds." What are ways in which we see Daunis acting to keep her worlds separate? Do you think she feels a stronger connection to one world or the other? Do you agree it's easier to keep worlds separate?

3. Daunis often seeks wisdom and guidance from the Elders. How does the role of the Elders compare to the role of senior citizens in your community?

4. Both Daunis and Jamie struggle with their identities—while Daunis feels torn between many, Jamie doesn't have any sense of where he comes from. Are there similarities in the way they consider their identities? Differences?

5. Aunt Teddie describes a Blanket Party as "Nish Kwe justice." What do you think of this form of justice and how Blanket Parties were created? How do you think this might influence Daunis's understanding of justice?

6. Teddie tells Daunis, "Not every Elder is a cultural teacher and not all cultural teachers are Elders. It's okay to listen to what people say and only hold onto the parts that resonate with you. It's okay to leave the rest behind. Trust yourself to know the difference." What does Teddie mean? What does Daunis choose to hold onto and leave behind from her culture?

7. Describe Daunis's feelings after she learns that her testimony can't be used in the court. Why do you believe the author made this choice?

8. Why did the author choose to end the story on a powwow scene? How does this speak to the themes of the book?

9. Daunis references the Seven Grandfather teachings throughout the novel—Love, Humility, Respect, Honesty, Bravery, Wisdom, and Truth. Are there characters or moments that help Daunis learn and embody these teachings?

MAD, BAD & DANGEROUS TO KNOW
Samira Ahmed

It's August in Paris and 17-year-old Khayyam Maquet—American, French, Indian, Muslim—is at a crossroads. This holiday with her parents should be a dream trip for the budding art historian. But her maybe-ex-boyfriend is probably ghosting her, she might have just blown her chance at getting into her dream college, and now all she really wants is to be back home in Chicago figuring out her messy life instead of brooding in the City of Light.

Two hundred years before Khayyam's summer of discontent, Leila is struggling to survive and keep her true love hidden from the Pasha who has "gifted" her with favored status in his harem. In the present day—and with the company of Alex, a très charming teen descendant of Alexandre Dumas—Khayyam immerses herself in the search for a rumored lost painting, uncovering a connection between Leila and Alexandre Dumas, Eugène Delacroix, and Lord Byron that may have been erased from history.

Echoing across centuries, Leila and Khayyam's lives intertwine, and as one woman's long-forgotten life is uncovered, another's is transformed.

"A smart, feminist holiday romance, asking some pointed questions about whose voices are honoured by history." —***The Guardian***

"A delightful romp through the City of Light ... examines issues of cultural identity and racism both as they existed in the past and still manifest today." —**NPR.org**

"A sweeping, feminist novel about equality and identity." —***Teen Vogue***

ABOUT THE AUTHOR: **Samira Ahmed** was born in Bombay, India, and grew up in a small town in Illinois in a house that smelled like fried onions, cardamom, and potpourri. A graduate of the University of Chicago, she's lived in Vermont, Chicago, New York City, and Kauai, where she spent a year searching for the perfect mango. Follow her on Twitter and Instagram @sam_aye_ahm.

April 2020 | Hardcover | $18.99 | 9781616959890 | Soho Teen

CONVERSATION STARTERS

1. Khayyam's very first words to the reader are, "I live in between spaces." Why does she feel that way? How do those words foreshadow one of the novel's themes?

2. Why does Leila hate the title of "haseki" when it means "the favored"? And how does her first chapter foreshadow her destiny—both while she was alive and after her death?

3. Khayyam, Leila, Alexandre, Zaid, Byron, and Dumas all conceal things or tell lies. What are the different prices they pay for their lies? Are some lies justified? Do some lies "weigh" more than others?

4. Why is Khayyam hesitant about sharing Leila's story with the world when she and Alexandre finally start discovering the real truth? Why does she change her mind? Was that the right choice?

5. Who decides what history is written and what stories are pushed aside? How does racism and patriarchy play a role in that? What criteria would you use to decide what stories and accomplishments deserve to be known and remembered?

6. Why does Leila tell Byron, "I have much more to fear from men than jinn"? Does that ring true in her life?

7. Different men tried to use Khayyam and Leila as means to their desired ends. How do Khayyam and Leila fight that?

8. Khayyam and Leila lived in very different times but both struggle to find their voice and tell their own story. What similar forces were they fighting against? What societal change allowed Khayyam to have more freedoms than Leila? How did she choose to use that power and privilege? Why does Leila choose to finally write her own story?

9. What is eternal return? How does it play out in the novel? Is it real?

ReadingGroupChoices.com

ON THESE MAGIC SHORES
Yamile Saied Méndez

Minerva must take care of her sisters after her mother's disappearance in this magical novel for young readers by an up-and-coming Latina author.

Twelve-year-old Minerva Soledad Miranda is determined to reach her goals, despite shouldering more responsibility than the other kids at school — like caring for her two sisters while her mom works two jobs. But one night, Minerva's mom doesn't come home, and Minerva has to figure out what to do. Was Mamá snapped up by ICE? Will the girls be sent to foster homes or holding centers for migrant kids? Minerva and her sisters can't let anyone know Mamá has disappeared. They'll just pretend everything is normal until she comes back.

Minerva's plan falls apart the first afternoon, when her baby sister throws a tantrum during Minerva's audition for *Peter Pan*. But as the days pass and Minerva grows ever more worried about her mother, something magical seems to be watching out for them. Eventually, Minerva must make the hardest choice of her life. And when she does, she'll be prepared to face life's challenges — with friendship, hope, and a little bit of fairy magic.

"Méndez tackles problems of racism, discrimination, income inequality, immigration, and ethnic and cultural stereotypes. There is much to like, and readers will find a strong and resilient character they can root for." —**Kirkus Reviews**

ABOUT THE AUTHOR: **Yamile (sha-MEE-lay) Saied Méndez** is a fútbol-obsessed Argentine American author who loves meteor showers, summer, astrology, and pizza. She lives in Utah with her Puerto Rican husband and their five kids, two adorable dogs, and one majestic cat. An inaugural Water Dean Myers Grant and a New Visions Award Honor recipient, she's also a graduate of Voices of Our Nations (VONA) and the Vermont College of Fine Arts MFA in Writing for Children and Young Adult program. Find her online at yamilesmendez.com.

June 2020 | Hardcover | $19.95 | 9781643790312 | Lee & Low Books

CONVERSATION STARTERS

1. Minerva's family kept traditions from Argentina as we see when they drink mate, leave milk for the peques, or wait for El Ratón Pérez instead of the Tooth Fairy. What are some traditions that your family has kept for generations?

2. Minerva acts like her sisters' second mom out of the family's lack of social network. But what are some instances in which she shows she's still very much a child in her heart?

3. Why is Minerva so perturbed when she discovers that the blue dress her mother gave her for the play's audition was formerly owned by Bailey Cooper?

4. Why is Maverick curious about Minerva, her family, and her culture? What is he hoping to learn for himself?

5. Why is Minerva troubled by the part she wins in *Peter Pan*? Do you agree with the actions she eventually takes to challenge the role? Why or why not?

6. The play and book *Peter Pan* portray a beloved story that still shows harmful representation of different groups. Why is it important to examine beloved stories for stereotypes and hurtful language? How do we balance the love of these stories and the archetypes they represent with the need to point out their failures?

7. Why doesn't Minerva tell anyone her mother has disappeared? If you were in Minerva's shoes, what would you do?

8. Minerva and her sisters are U.S. citizens. Why do the girls worry about possibly being picked up by ICE?

9. When Minerva is stopped by the neighborhood police officer, why do you think the officer is suspicious of her? When the boys come out to help, how do you feel about the interactions that follow?

10. Why do you think Minerva's mother would refuse help from neighbors?

ONE OF THE GOOD ONES
Maika and Maritza Moulite

A shockingly powerful exploration of the lasting impact of prejudice and indomitable spirit of sisterhood that will have readers questioning what it truly means to be an ally, from sister-writer duo Maika Moulite and Maritza Moulite, authors of *Dear Haiti, Love Alaine*.

Isn't being human enough?

When teen social activist and history buff Kezi Smith is killed under mysterious circumstances after attending a social justice rally, her devastated sister Happi and their family are left reeling in the aftermath. As Kezi becomes another immortalized victim in the fight against police brutality, Happi begins to question the idealized way her sister is remembered. Perfect. Angelic.

One of the good ones.

Even as the phrase rings wrong in her mind—why are only certain people deemed worthy to be missed?—Happi and her sister Genny embark on a journey to honor Kezi in their own way, using an heirloom copy of *The Negro Motorist Green Book* as their guide. But there's a twist to Kezi's story that no one could've ever expected—one that will change everything all over again.

ABOUT THE AUTHORS: **Maika Moulite** is a Miami native and the daughter of Haitian immigrants. She earned a bachelor's in marketing from Florida State University and an MBA from the University of Miami. When she's not using her digital prowess to help nonprofits and major organizations tell their stories online, she's sharpening her skills as a PhD student at Howard University. She's the eldest of four sisters and loves young adult fantasy, fierce female leads, and laughing.

Maritza Moulite graduated from the University of Florida with a bachelor's in women's studies and the University of Southern California with a master's in journalism. She's worked in various capacities for NBC News, CNN and *USA TODAY*. An admirer of Michelle Obama, Maritza is a PhD student at the University of Pennsylvania exploring ways to improve literacy in under-resourced communities. Her favorite song is "September" by Earth, Wind & Fire.

January 2020 | Hardcover | $18.99 | 9781335145802 | Inkyard Press

CONVERSATION STARTERS

1. How does each character's race impact their awareness of the world around them? How do they have to think about both physical and emotional safety?

2. The refrain of "one of the good ones" is evident throughout this book. What does this phrase mean? Kezi was described as "one of the good ones" and Shaqueria was not. How did the world react to their arrests and subsequent events?

3. What does Kezi value about herself, and how does that align (or not) with what her parents value about her, and what her sisters value? How does that contrast with what society values?

4. The Smith family is going through a time of profound grief. How are they each reacting to it and channeling it? What are the pressures from society on how they channel their grief?

5. Describe how the three sisters react differently to growing up in the same household and in society. How do these differences affect the way they interact with each other?

6. Guilt manifests itself in a variety of ways throughout the book. Give examples of ways in which Kezi, Happi, and Genny express guilt and how their guilt drives and influences their actions.

7. How do the actions of the past shape the narrative of the present? In what ways are the characters aware of this legacy, and how do they react to it? Are there times when they have to change and adapt from it? How does a character's race affect the way that these legacies are passed down?

8. How does Kezi's relationship with Ximena intersect with her relationship with her family and with how she is viewed in society?

9. Discuss what allyship looks like in *One of the Good Ones* in terms of supporting the Black community and the LGBTQ+ community. How does that intersect in real life?

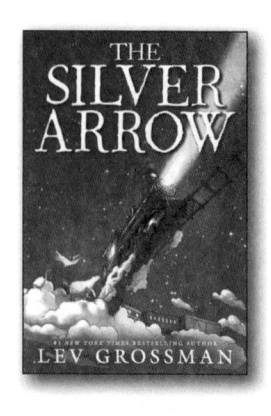

THE SILVER ARROW
Lev Grossman

From the #1 *New York Times* bestselling author of *The Magicians* comes a must-read, wholly original middle-grade debut perfect for fans of *The Chronicles of Narnia* and Roald Dahl.

Kate and her younger brother Tom lead dull, uninteresting lives. And if their dull, uninteresting parents are anything to go by, they don't have much to look forward to. Why can't Kate have thrilling adventures and save the world the way people do in books? Even her 11th birthday is shaping up to be mundane – that is, until her mysterious and highly irresponsible Uncle Herbert, whom she's never even met before, surprises her with the most unexpected, exhilarating, inappropriate birthday present of all time: a colossal steam locomotive called the Silver Arrow.

Kate and Tom's parents want to send it right back where it came from. But Kate and Tom have other ideas – and so does the Silver Arrow – and soon they're off to distant lands along magical rail lines in the company of an assortment of exotic animals who, it turns out, can talk. With only curiosity, excitement, their own resourcefulness and the thrill of the unknown to guide them, Kate and Tom are on the adventure of a lifetime ... and who knows? They just might end up saving the world after all.

This thrilling fantasy adventure will not only entertain young readers but inspire them to see the beautiful, exciting, and precious world around them with new eyes.

"A perfect book to cuddle up with and savor—and even better to read aloud with someone you love." —**Adam Gidwitz, bestselling and Newbery honor-winning author of** *A Tale Dark and Grimm* **and** *The Inquisitor's Tale*

ABOUT THE AUTHOR: **Lev Grossman** is the author of five novels including the #1 *New York Times* bestselling Magicians trilogy, which has been published in 30 countries. A TV adaptation of the trilogy is now in its fifth season as the top-rated show on Syfy. Grossman is also an award-winning journalist who spent 15 years as the book critic and lead technology writer at *Time* magazine. He lives in New York City with his wife and three children.

September 2020 | Hardcover | $16.99 | 9780316539531 |
Little, Brown Books for Young Readers

CONVERSATION STARTERS

1. If you could have any birthday present in the world, what would you wish for? Why?

2. Do you think technology makes it easier or harder for people to stay connected, both to other people and the world around them?

3. Grace Hopper, the famous inventor and computer programmer, is one of Kate's biggest role models. Who are some of your role models? Why do they inspire you?

4. If you were the conductor of a magical train like the Silver Arrow, which train cars would you choose to add? Why?

5. Which animal did you most enjoy learning about? What was your favorite fact about them?

6. Over the course of the book, Kate learns about invasive species from the animals. How do invasive species impact other animals and their environments? How are humans an invasive species?

7. What examples of changing habitats are shown or described throughout the book? How do these changes affect the animals who live there?

8. Kate and Tom spend time as trees in exchange for wood to fuel the Silver Arrow. How does being a tree feel to them? How do you think being another form of life would feel?

9. Kate notes that, "People looked down on animals, but animals never made excuses or felt sorry for themselves". (p 183) What other differences between animals and humans do Kate and Tom notice? How are Kate and Tom's interactions with the animals in the book different from other classic children's books? Do you think our relationship with the natural world has changed? How?

10. When describing the plight of the baby pangolin Kate says, "Some problems in this world just don't have answers. Not yet." (p 216) How can we work to find answers for those problems? What can you do personally to make our world a better place?

STAMPED: RACISM, ANTIRACISM, AND YOU
Jason Reynolds and Ibram X. Kendi

This #1 *New York Times* bestseller and *USA Today* bestseller is a timely, crucial, and empowering exploration of racism — and antiracism — in America.

This is NOT a history book. This is a book about the here and now. A book to help us better understand why we are where we are. A book about race.

The construct of race has always been used to gain and keep power, to create dynamics that separate and silence. This remarkable reimagining of Dr. Ibram X. Kendi's National Book Award-winning *Stamped from the Beginning* reveals the history of racist ideas in America, and inspires hope for an antiracist future. It takes you on a race journey from then to now, shows you why we feel how we feel, and why the poison of racism lingers. It also proves that while racist ideas have always been easy to fabricate and distribute, they can also be discredited.

Through a gripping, fast-paced, and energizing narrative written by beloved award-winner Jason Reynolds, this book shines a light on the many insidious forms of racist ideas—and on ways readers can identify and stamp out racist thoughts in their daily lives.

"*Stamped is the book I wish I had as a young person and am so grateful my own children have now.*" —**Jacqueline Woodson, bestselling and National Book Award-winning author of** *Brown Girl Dreaming*

"*Reynolds's engaging, clear prose shines a light on difficult and confusing subjects.... This is no easy feat.*" —**The New York Times Book Review**

ABOUT THE AUTHORS: Jason Reynolds is the #1 *New York Times* bestselling author of many books. He is a two-time National Book Award finalist; the recipient of a Newbery Honor, a Printz Honor, and multiple Coretta Scott King Honors; and the winner of a Kirkus Prize, two Walter Dean Myers Awards, and an NAACP Image Award, among other honors.

Ibram X. Kendi is a #1 *New York Times* bestselling author, professor of history and international studies, and the Director of the Boston University Center for Antiracist Research.

March 2020 | Hardcover | $18.99 | 9780316453691 |
Little, Brown Books for Young Readers

CONVERSATION STARTERS

1. The first chapter defines segregationists, assimilationists, and antiracists. Were you familiar with these terms before you read *Stamped*? Did your understanding of these words change by the end?

2. What are examples of racism that you've encountered or experienced? Referencing the list of racist ideas in Chapter 6, explain why and how your personal experiences with racism are tied to racist ideas that are hundreds of years old.

3. As seen with movies like *Tarzan, Planet of the Apes*, and *Rocky*, pop culture and media have played a large role in reinforcing racist ideas, whether their stories are overtly racist or are a bit sneakier in their propagation of racist ideas. What current movies, TV shows, and stories promote racist ideas, and how?

4. How do race, gender, and sexual orientation intersect and create different barriers for queer women of color?

5. Why is Angela Davis a champion of antiracist thought and practice? Discuss the ways in which Davis fought for antiracism at different points in her life.

6. The authors note how Richard Nixon would demean Black people in his speeches without ever saying "Black" and "White" by using words like "urban" and "ghetto". (p 191-192) What are other ways we invoke race without overtly mentioning race?

7. Abraham Lincoln, W.E.B. Du Bois, and Booker T. Washington are remembered as defenders of Black liberation. How did these figures propel antiracist thought and enforce racist ideas? Can a person have racist, segregationist, and antiracist ideas all at once? How?

8. Jason Reynolds introduces the concept of double consciousness: "A two-ness. A self that is Black and a self that is American". (p 124) Why might people of color feel this way?

9. Though published as a book for young people, how do readers of all ages benefit from *Stamped*?

10. What surprised you in this book? What angered you or made you sad? What other emotions did you experience while reading?

11. After finishing *Stamped*, how do you feel about the history of racism? What habits and actions can you implement to promote antiracism?

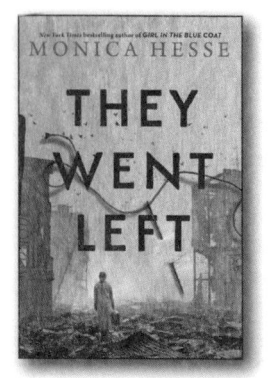

THEY WENT LEFT
Monica Hesse

The acclaimed *New York Times* bestselling tour de force historical mystery from Monica Hesse, the award-winning author of *Girl in the Blue Coat*

Germany, 1945. The soldiers who liberated the Gross-Rosen concentration camp said the war was over, but nothing feels over to 18-year-old Zofia Lederman.

Her body has barely begun to heal, her mind feels broken. And her life is completely shattered: Three years ago, she and her younger brother, Abek, were the only members of their family to be sent to the right, away from the gas chambers of Auschwitz-Birkenau. Everyone else—her parents, her grandmother, radiant Aunt Maja—they went left.

Zofia's last words to her brother were a promise: *Abek to Zofia, A to Z. When I find you again, we will fill our alphabet.* Now her journey to fulfill that vow takes her through Poland and Germany where everyone she meets is trying to piece together a future from a painful past. But the deeper Zofia digs, the more impossible her search seems. How can she find one boy in a sea of the missing?

"Hesse writes with tenderness and insight about the stories we tell ourselves in order to survive and the ways we cobble together family with whatever we have. When the plot twists come, they are gut punches—some devastating, others offering hope ... Crucial." —*New York Times Book Review*

"A heartbreaking, gorgeously written story ... The ending left me breathless and awed by its expression of enduring love." —**Jewell Parker Rhodes,** *New York Times* **bestselling author of** *Ghost Boys*

ABOUT THE AUTHOR: **Monica Hesse** is the bestselling author of *Girl in the Blue Coat*, *American Fire*, and *The War Outside*, as well as a columnist at *The Washington Post*. She lives outside Washington, D.C. with her husband and their dog.

April 2020 | Hardcover | $17.99 | 9780316490573 |
Little, Brown Books for Young Readers

CONVERSATION STARTERS

1. Zofia wrestles with her own memories over the course of her search for Abek. How does the Sosnowiec of Zofia's memories compare to the Sosnowiec she returns to?

2. How do physical possessions, particularly clothing, anchor Zofia and other characters to the present? To the past?

3. Zofia speaks of the "small acts of defiance" braved by people in the camps. (p 209) How do characters assert their humanity in the face of the systematic Nazi efforts to dehumanize them?

4. What role does storytelling play in preserving the legacy of survivors and their families? How do records of survivors' stories, both written and oral, inform Zofia's search for Abek?

5. Zofia suggests that "the absence of pain is not the same as the presence of happiness". (p 198) How do survivors move forward? What moments of happiness in the face of pain does Zofia witness or experience?

6. What does family come to mean to Zofia and the other survivors she encounters? How does this definition change?

7. What do different characters do to survive both during and after the war? How do they reckon with those actions as they recover? How does survivors' guilt affect them?

8. In the aftermath of the war, what systems and forces rise up to establish order from the chaos? What are Zofia's experiences with these systems? How does Foehrenwald reflect the larger post-war state of Europe?

9. Throughout the book, Zofia references the alphabet she embroidered on the inside of Abek's coat. How do the names and places that make up this alphabet persist in Zofia's memory? How does she distinguish truth in these memories from fabrications?

10. In her author's note, Monica Hesse notes that "the war didn't end people's prejudice." What instances of anti-Semitism does Zofia encounter in her post-war journey?

11. Do you resonate with any one particular character? Why?

12. Do you see similarities between post-war Europe and our world today? How can we benefit from the knowledge of history?

THIS IS MY AMERICA
Kim Johnson

The Hate U Give meets *Just Mercy* in this unflinching yet uplifting first novel that explores the racist injustices in the American justice system.

Every week, seventeen-year-old Tracy Beaumont writes letters to Innocence X, asking the organization to help her father, an innocent Black man on death row. After seven years, Tracy is running out of time—her dad has only 267 days left. Then the unthinkable happens. The police arrive in the night, and Tracy's older brother, Jamal, goes from being a bright, promising track star to a "thug" on the run, accused of killing a white girl. Determined to save her brother, Tracy investigates what really happened between Jamal and Angela down at the Pike. But will Tracy and her family survive the uncovering of skeletons of their Texas town's racist history that still haunt the present?

Fans of Nic Stone, Karen M. McManus, Holly Jackson, and Jason Reynolds won't want to miss this provocative and gripping debut.

"An incredible and searing examination of the often tragic collision of racism and a flawed criminal justice system. Read and reread ... and reread again."
—**Nic Stone**, #1 *New York Times* bestselling author of *Dear Martin*

ABOUT THE AUTHOR: **Kim Johnson** held leadership positions in social justice organizations as a teen. She's now a college administrator who maintains civic engagement throughout the community while also mentoring Black student activists and leaders. *This Is My America* is her debut novel. It explores racial injustice against innocent Black men who are criminally sentenced and the families left behind to pick up the pieces. She holds degrees from the University of Oregon and the University of Maryland, College Park. Kim lives her best life in Oregon with her husband and two kids. Find her at kcjohnsonwrites.com and follow her on Twitter and Instagram @kcjohnsonwrites.

July 2020 | Hardcover | $17.99 | 9780593118764 |
Random House Books for Young Readers

CONVERSATION STARTERS

1. What does the title mean to you? Complete this sentence: My America is...

2. When the sheriff refers to Jamas as "boy", Tracy reflects, "The word 'boy' keeps running in my head. A bitter taste flushes in my mouth, the way that world drawls out like just another slur in coded language". (p 70) What are the connotations of the word "boy"? What does Tracy mean by "coded language"?

3. Compare the experiences of Jackson Ridges, Daddy Greg, and Tracy's father. How do their experiences living under the prison-industrial complex affect them and their families?

4. After Angela's murder, the school brings in grief counselors. (p 109) Compare public and private mourning in the book. Who is most likely to be publicly mourned, and why?

5. Reflect on the chapter title "Guilty ... Until Proven Innocent". Discuss if the presumption of innocent until proven guilty applies equally across race and class. In what ways do Black men experience interactions with the police that might differ by race and gender.

6. How do characters in the book cope with their trauma?

7. What motivates characters to solve the mystery? Discuss Tracy's process for gathering evidence. Why is it risky? Why is it necessary?

8. Why does Johnson choose to omit Jamal's version of events from the story for most of the narrative?

9. Why does Richard Brighton yell "gun!"? (p 360) Who had the benefit of the doubt in this scene? In what ways might the response have been different if Jamal and Angela switched roles in the story?

10. How do the characters differ in the ways they "work for justice"?

11. Consider the role of media in the book. How is it helpful or harmful? Whose interests does the media serve?

12. Tracy quotes Dr. King in one of her letters to Innocence X. "The arc of the moral universe is long, but it bends towards justice." Do you agree with Dr. King's vision? Is Johnson's ending hopeful?

13. What is Johnson's commentary on racism?

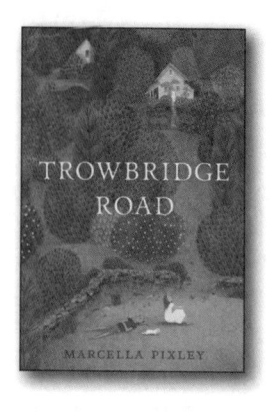

TROWBRIDGE ROAD
Marcella Pixley

In a stunning novel set in the 1980s, a girl with heavy secrets awakens her sleepy street to the complexities of love and courage.

It's the summer of '83 on Trowbridge Road, and June Bug Jordan is hungry. Months after her father's death from complications from AIDS, her mother has stopped cooking and refuses to leave the house, instead locking herself away to scour at the germs she believes are everywhere. June Bug threatens this precarious existence by going out into the neighborhood, gradually befriending Ziggy, an imaginative boy who is living with his Nana Jean after experiencing troubles of his own. But as June Bug's connection to the world grows stronger, her mother's grows more distant — even dangerous — pushing June Bug to choose between truth and healing and the only home she has ever known.

Trowbridge Road paints an unwavering portrait of a girl and her family touched by mental illness and grief. Set in the Boston suburbs during the first years of the AIDS epidemic, the novel explores how a seemingly perfect neighborhood can contain restless ghosts and unspoken secrets. Written with deep insight and subtle lyricism by acclaimed author Marcella Pixley, *Trowbridge Road* demonstrates our power to rescue one another even when our hearts are broken.

"June Bug narrates this work of historical realism with a magical, poetic quality, turning the ordinary extraordinary. June Bug and Ziggy's fanciful adventures are likely to resonate with fans of Katherine Paterson's Bridge to Terabithia *... An exceptional story for readers who feel deeply." —*Kirkus Reviews *(starred review)*

ABOUT THE AUTHOR: **Marcella Pixley** is the author of three books for young adults, including *Ready to Fall*. She has been nominated for a Pushcart Prize for poetry and earned a master's from Bread Loaf School of English at Middlebury College. She teaches writing to middle-schoolers in Massachusetts, where she lives with her family.

October 2020 | Hardcover | $17.99 | 9781536207507 | Candlewick Press

CONVERSATION STARTERS

1. The author has set this book in 1983. What details does she include that make you realize that it is not a contemporary setting?

2. June Bug and Ziggy both have someone in their lives who cares for them when their mothers can't. June Bug has her uncle Toby, and Ziggy has his grandmother, Nana Jean. Compare and contrast the ways in which the two take care of the children.

3. In the chapter "Rules for Staying Clean", we learn about the rules that June Bug's mother follows to keep germs away from them. (p 46) What did you think when you read them? If you were June Bug, what would you do?

4. When there is a neighborhood cookout at the house across from Nana Jean's, Ziggy and June Bug watch everyone eating, chatting, and playing. After watching the girl across the street, Heather Anne, having a great time on the swing, June Bug suddenly throws a rock at her. Why do you think she does this?

5. June Bug packs what she calls "necessaries" into her backpack so she can always keep herself clean enough for her mother. The backpack becomes very significant in her life, and she refers to it as if it were alive. What do you think it means to June Bug?

6. Nana Jean once told Ziggy, referring to his mother, "Sometimes they love you, but they don't know how to make it stick". (p 137) What does she mean by that?

7. The day after Jenny helps June Bug bury her mother's ruined clothes, we learn that Nana Jean had not had as smooth a life as we had assumed. Does this change what you think about Nana Jean? About Jenny?

8. Both Ziggy and June Bug have secrets they hold inside that are really too big for a kid to deal with alone. How do they determine which adults to trust?

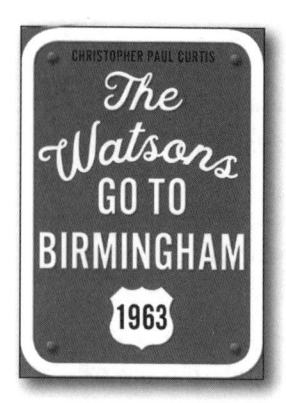

THE WATSONS GO TO BIRMINGHAM – 1963
Christopher Paul Curtis

Celebrate the 25th anniversary of this Newbery and Coretta Scott King Honoree about a hilarious family on a road trip at one of the most important times in America's history. This special edition makes a perfect gift and includes bonus content.

Enter the hilarious world of ten-year-old Kenny and his family, the Weird Watsons of Flint, Michigan. There's Momma, Dad, little sister Joetta, and brother Byron, who's thirteen and an "official juvenile delinquent."

When Byron gets to be too much trouble, they head South to Birmingham to visit Grandma, the one person who can shape him up. And they'll be in Birmingham during one of the darkest moments in America's history.

"Marvelous ... both comic and deeply moving." —*The New York Times*

"This is a book that changes lives. It certainly changed mine." —**Kate DiCamillo**, author of *Because of Winn-Dixie* and *The Tale of Despereaux*

"One of the best novels EVER." —**Jacqueline Woodson**, author of *Brown Girl Dreaming* and *Harbor Me*

ABOUT THE AUTHOR: **Christopher Paul Curtis** is the author of *The Watsons Go to Birmingham—1963*, one of the most highly acclaimed first novels for young readers in recent years. It was singled out for many awards, among them a Newbery Honor and a Coretta Scott King Honor, and has been a bestseller in hardcover and paperback. Christopher grew up in Flint, Michigan. After high school he began working on the assembly line at the Fisher Body Flint Plant No. 1 while attending the Flint branch of the University of Michigan. He is now a full-time writer, and lives with his family in Windsor, Ontario.

November 2020 | Paperback | $11.99 | 9780593306499 |
Yearling Books from Random House Children's Books

CONVERSATION STARTERS

1. At what point in the novel does Curtis introduce the conflict to create the tension in the story?

2. What is the climax, or the turning point, of *The Watsons Go to Birmingham—1963*, that changes the outcome of the plot?

3. How does the church bombing change Kenny and Byron's relationship?

4. How does Mrs. Watson sense that something is wrong between Kenny and Rufus? Kenny thinks that Rufus changed while the Watsons were away. Do you think it's Rufus or Kenny who changed?

5. Why does Mrs. Watson think that Grandma Sands is the person who can change Byron's behavior? Describe Kenny's reaction when he meets his grandmother for the first time. Why does Kenny think that Byron will win the battle with Grandma Sands? At what point does he realize that he is wrong?

6. Kenny worries that he won't ever know how to be a grown-up. Mr. Watson assures his son that he'll have lots of time to practice before he actually becomes a grown-up. Describe his baby steps and giant steps toward becoming a man.

7. Kenny struggles to understand how anyone could bomb a church and kill four little girls. Discuss the following comment from Byron: "I don't think they're sick at all, I think they just let hate eat them up and turn them into monsters." How does Byron's perception of the bombers apply to those responsible for violent acts in our current society?

8. Kenny tells Byron, "I'm not scared, I'm just real, real ashamed of myself." Why is he ashamed? How does Byron help Kenny come to terms with his shame?

9. The novel is told in first person from Kenny's point of view. How does Curtis use dialogue to reveal what other characters are thinking?

WHAT MAKES US
Rafi Mittlefehldt

A viral video reveals a teen's dark family history, leaving him to reckon with his heritage, legacy, and identity in this fiery, conversation-starting novel.

Eran Sharon knows nothing of his father except that he left when Eran was a baby. Now a senior in high school and living with his protective but tight-lipped mother, Eran is a passionate young man deeply interested in social justice and equality. When he learns that the Houston police have launched a program to increase traffic stops, Eran organizes a peaceful protest. But a heated moment at the protest goes viral, and a reporter connects the Sharon family to a tragedy fifteen years earlier — and asks if Eran is anything like his father, a supposed terrorist. Soon enough, Eran is wondering the same thing, especially when the people he's gone to school and temple with for years start to look at him differently. Timely, powerful, and full of nuance, Rafi Mittlefehldt's sophomore novel confronts the prejudices, fears, and strengths of family and community, striking right to the heart of what makes us who we are.

"Mittlefehldt's thoughtful, nuanced exploration of identity pulled me in from the very first page, and I could barely put it down. Most important, this book provides satisfying, much-needed representation of a contemporary, complex Jewish teen and his family." —**Lisa Rosinsky, author of** *Inevitable and Only*

"This coming-of-age story has heft—and much relevance. Strong medicine for readers interested in how society accepts or rejects those who are different." —*School Library Journal*

ABOUT THE AUTHOR: **Rafi Mittlefehldt** is the author of two young adult novels, *What Makes Us* and *It Looks Like This*. Raised in Houston, he worked briefly as a reporter for a small-town newspaper in Central Texas before settling in New York. He now lives in Philadelphia with his husband Damien and dog Betty.

October 2019 | Hardcover | $17.99 | 9780763697501 | Candlewick Press
May 2021 | Paperback | $8.99 | 9781536219050 | Candlewick Press

CONVERSATION STARTERS

1. Describe Eema's personality and the relationship between Eran and Eema early in the book. How does their relationship change over the course of the novel? Explain why Eema didn't tell Eran about his father and their past. Why do people believe that Eema must have known what Dani was planning?

2. After Eema takes him from the demonstration, Eran describes his feelings, including "Anger, of course, always anger". (p 47) Discuss the role of anger in his life and his relationship with his mother. Why does he believe anger can be useful, "that it gets stuff done"? (p 283)

3. Eema tells Eran that his father often quoted from the Talmud, referring to a passage that says "if someone has power to prevent injustice but does not, then he is responsible for this injustice". (p 154) Do you agree with that idea?

4. The topic of Eran's anger and how it relates to his father's anger comes up when he, Jade, and Declan are in the concrete pipe. Discuss Jade's observation that anger can be a virtue and her two questions: "Isn't that what makes us, anyway? What we decide, rather than what we're born into?". (p 284) Relate her comment to the book's title and to her own circumstances. Why will Jade "think about this moment years later"?

5. What is the effect of having some chapters focus on Jade? What aspects of her story parallel Eran's? What aspects contrast with his? Why are the chapters about Jade written in third person and those about Eran in first person?

6. What role has the synagogue played in Eran's and Eema's lives? Discuss some of the reactions at the synagogue when Eran and Eema go there in chapter twelve. Why does Zack say, "Jews don't get to speak without thinking, Eran."? (p 219) Describe the attack on the synagogue and the responses of various people, including Eran, his mother, and his friends.

7. What are some of the ways that journalists are portrayed in this novel? Why does Benson Domani write the story connecting Eema, Eran, and Dani? How does he justify writing it? Why does Eran's mother think they shouldn't speak with reporters? What are the consequences when Eran does speak with them? Discuss the scene at the gas station and the role of the reporters there.

ReadingGroupChoices.com

BOOK GROUP FAVORITES FROM 2019

We asked thousands of book groups to tell us what books they read and discussed during 2019 that they enjoyed most. The top titles were:

FICTION	NONFICTION	YOUNG ADULT
The Great Alone Kristin Hannah	St Martin's Press	*The Radium Girls* Kate Moore	Sourcebooks	*The Hate U Give* Angie Thomas	Balzer + Bray
An American Marriage Tayari Jones	Algonquin Books	*Killers of the Flower Moon* David Grann	Vintage	**TIE** *Dear Evan Hansen* Val Emmich, Steven Levenson, Benj Pasek & Justin Paul	LBYR
TIE *The Tattooist of Auschwitz* Heather Morris	Harper Paperbacks	*Educated* Tara Westover	Random House	*The Poet X* Elizabeth Acevedo	HarperTeen
The Underground Railroad Colson Whitehead	Anchor	*Hillbilly Elegy* J.D. Vance	Harper Paperbacks	*I Am Not Your Perfect Mexican Daughter* Erika Sánchez	Ember
The Book Woman of Troublesome Creek Kim Michele Richardson	Sourcebooks	*Becoming* Michelle Obama	Crown	*Fountains of Silence* Ruta Sepetys	Philomel Books
Carnegie's Maid Marie Benedict	Sourcebooks	*Fly Girls* Keith O'Brien	HMH	*The Book Thief* Markus Zusak	Alfred A. Knopf
Sold on a Monday Kristina McMorris	Sourcebooks	*The Stranger in the Woods* Michael Finkel	Vintage	**TIE** *Geekerella* Ashley Poston	Quirk Books
A Gentleman in Moscow Amor Towles	Viking	*Women Rowing North* Mary Pipher	Bloomsbury USA	*Love, Hate and Other Filters* Samira Ahmed	Soho Teen
The Stars Are Fire Anita Shreve	Vintage	*Just Mercy* Bryan Stevenson	Spiegel & Grau	
	Being Mortal Atul Gawande	Picador	

Please visit ReadingGroupChoices.com between January 1 and April 1, 2021 to enter our 2020 Favorite Books Contest by telling us about your favorite books of 2020. You will be entered for a chance to win bookstore gift certificates to use toward your meetings plus books for each person in your group, compliments of our publishing partners.

READING GROUP CHOICES

Selections for Lively Discussions

GUIDELINES FOR LIVELY BOOK DISCUSSIONS

1. RESPECT SPACE - Avoid "crosstalk" or talking over others.
2. ALLOW SPACE - Some of us are more outgoing and others more reserved. If you've had a chance to talk, allow others time to offer their thoughts as well.
3. BE OPEN - Keep an open mind, learn from others, and acknowlege there are differences in opinon. That's what makes it interesting!
4. OFFER NEW THOUGHTS - Try not to repeat what others have said, but offer a new perspective.
5. STAY ON THE TOPIC - Contribute to the flow of conversation by holding your comments to the topic of the book, keeping personal references to an appropriate medium.

Great Books ∼ Great People ∼ Great Conversation

DO YOU LOVE TO READ?

Spread the joy of reading and build a sense of community by starting a Little Free Library book exchange!

Hailed by the *New York Times* as "a global sensation", Little Free Library book exchanges are "take a book, return a book" gathering places where neighbors share their favorite literature and stories.

LITTLE FREE LIBRARY.ORG ®
TAKE A BOOK • RETURN A BOOK

Find locations near you and learn how to start your own at *www.littlefreelibrary.org*

INTRODUCING THE NEXT GREAT AUTHOR

Indies Introduce.
It's what independent booksellers have been doing forever – discovering and championing new authors.

INDIES Introduce

See titles at
BookWeb.org/indiesintroduce

READING GROUP CHOICES

READING GROUP CHOICES' ADVISORY BOARD

Charlie Mead owned and managed Reading Group Choices from 2005 until 2014. He sold the business to Mary Morgan in April 2014. Charlie's business partner and wife, Barbara Drummond Mead, co-owned and managed the business until her passing in 2011. From 1972 to 1999, Charlie served at Digital Equipment Corporation (DEC) and Compaq Computer Corporation, both now part of Hewlett Packard, most recently as vice president of communication accounts worldwide. In 1999, Charlie became vice president of Sales of Interpath Communications Corporation, an Internet infrastructure company, until the company's sale in 2000. From 2000 to 2005, Charlie owned and managed Connxsys LLC, a communications consulting firm.

Donna Paz Kaufman founded Reading Group Choices in 1994 to connect publishers, booksellers, libraries, and readers with great books for group discussion. Today, Paz & Associates owns Story & Song Bookstore Bistro and continues to assist people around the globe open, manage, and sell their independent bookstores in The Bookstore Training Group. To learn more about Paz & Associates, visit PazBookBiz.com.

John Mutter is editor-in-chief of *Shelf Awareness*, the daily e-mail newsletter focusing on books, media about books, retailing and related issues to help booksellers, librarians and others do their jobs more effectively. Before he and his business partner, Jenn Risko, founded the company in May 2005, he was executive editor of bookselling at *Publishers Weekly*. He has covered book industry issues for 25 years and written for a variety of publications, including *The Bookseller* in the U.K.; *Australian Bookseller & Publisher*; *Boersenblatt*, the German book trade magazine; and *College Store Magazine* in the U.S. For more information about *Shelf Awareness*, go to its website, shelf-awareness.com.

Megan Hanson's background includes extensive customer service work, experience coordinating marketing campaigns for the Madrid-based NGO Colegas, plus serving as a Community Literacy Coordinator for the Madison non-profit Literacy Network. Since 2012, she has been working for the internationally-recognized non-profit Little Free Library, helping them to develop and scale to meet demand. Her focus is on digital marketing, data and web management, product development and customer service.

René Martin is the Events Director/Publicist at Quail Ridge Books in Raleigh, NC. "Nancy Olson, who owned and operated Quail Ridge Books & Music from 1981 until it was sold in 2013, hired me in 2000. I knew nothing about the book business, but said yes, it would be fun. And it has been! Sixteen years later I now know a little more about the book business, and love being the events coordinator/publicist for Quail Ridge Books. We now host almost 300 events a year. My goal is to make QRB a model publicity department, and we have a beautiful, new store in which to make that happen."

Nicole Sullivan opened BookBar, a community bookstore wine bar in 2013. Immediately recognizing a need to connect readers with book clubs in their area, she then founded bookclubhub.org in 2014. BookBed, an author bed & breakfast located just above the book store opened its doors in Fall of 2015. Additionally, she has funneled her passion for helping others to create successful bookstore / bar & cafe models through her work as a consultant with Paz & Associates. Nicole proudly serves as co-President and founder of her neighborhood business association, Tennyson Berkeley Business Association (TBBA) and as Treasurer of her local maintenance district for the city of Denver.

READING GROUP CHOICES ANNUAL GUIDES

Fiction, nonfiction, and young adult book recommendations are included in each annual edition.

Order online at www.ReadingGroupChoices.com

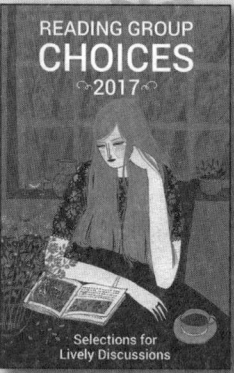